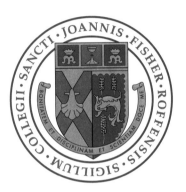

Lavery Library

St. John Fisher
College
Rochester, New York

# CAPTURED

*Tradition and Experience in*

# IN THE

*Contemporary Native American Writing*

# MIDDLE

# SIDNER
# LARSON

*A McLellan Book*

UNIVERSITY OF WASHINGTON PRESS

SEATTLE & LONDON

THIS BOOK IS PUBLISHED WITH THE ASSISTANCE OF A GRANT
FROM THE McLELLAN ENDOWED SERIES FUND,
ESTABLISHED THROUGH THE GENEROSITY OF
MARTHA McCLEARY McLELLAN & MARY McLELLAN WILLIAMS.

THE PAPER USED IN THIS PUBLICATION IS ACID FREE AND RECYCLED
FROM 10 PERCENT POST-CONSUMER AND AT LEAST 50 PERCENT
PRE-CONSUMER WASTE. IT MEETS THE MINIMUM REQUIREMENTS OF
THE AMERICAN NATIONAL STANDARD FOR INFORMATION SCIENCES
— PERMANENCE OF PAPER FOR PRINTED LIBRARY MATERIALS,
ANSI Z39.48-1984.

# CONTENTS

Introduction   3

House Made of Cards: The Construction of American Indians   2 1

American Indians, Authenticity, and the Future   3 9

Vine Deloria Jr.: Reconstructing the Logic of Belief   5 8

Constituting and Preserving Self through Writing   7 0

Louise Erdrich: Protecting and Celebrating Culture   7 8

James Welch's *Indian Lawyer*   1 0 4

Pragmatism and American Indian Thought   1 2 9

Conclusion   1 4 4

NOTES   1 5 7

BIBLIOGRAPHY   1 6 7

INDEX   1 7 5

# CAPTURED

*Tradition and Experience in*

# *IN THE*

*Contemporary Native American Writing*

# MIDDLE

# INTRODUCTION

AFTER SPENDING SUMMERS AT THE INDIAN reservation ranch where I was raised, after a ten-year stint in the whiskey trade, and after leaving the practice of law, I have always returned to school. As a young man I more than once found myself unhappy about my life and decided the best chance I had to do anything about it was to "go back to school," recognizing the potential of the educational process to create, change, and sustain attitudes and practices across cultures. I am particularly interested in relations between American Indian cultures and "mainstream," or "majority," culture, by which I mean those who primarily identify themselves with the largest groups of people, that is, whites, Americans, or Europeans.

I am intrigued by a transformative project that seeks to influence culture by means other than militant or nationalist approaches, such as the older American Indian conceptions of the Great Mystery as well as Keats's idea of negative capability, the power to remain open to mysteries, uncertainties, and doubts. This kind of thinking is a form of autobiography, a straining after self-knowledge where we both hate and love what we are discovering, where we continually recognize truths that attack other truths, where we do not understand ourselves too quickly.

Although education is the frame for my work, I am concerned that colleges and universities clearly encourage objective or disinterested learning, defining the organization of knowledge and inducting the young into society by inculcating certain values. A primary value is balancing the abstract ideas of education with consideration of what is actually happening in the lives of those with whom it seeks to interact. Conversely, the complete overshadowing of social attitudes by the social attitude of education itself, which seeks to suppress those who are different, cranky, or critical by placing them in a social context, should be avoided. Imagine the outrage of those who have set out to destroy that which they perceive as complacent and devitalizing in universities and in culture upon being redescribed by their enemies as "contributors to modern thought."

As part of this process, there are times lately when I feel like a missionary. It is a strange feeling — my lifework has evolved to a place of attempting to interpret to predominantly white middle-class students those American Indian worldviews that I believe may be helpful to them. In the context of American history, this is an inversion of the usual situation, where missionaries sought to "save" Indians. The reversal is dazzling to me, because it was just a short time ago that the American educational system went to some lengths to convince me that I would be lucky to make it through trade school. I now believe that almost anything can happen, even that we can teach people to stop killing each other and the environment.

Thinking about what good might result from this opportunity consistently leads me back to my childhood. Like the majority of Indian people, I have not had an easy life in most ways. It goes without saying that being Indian in the twentieth century is not easy; being part-Indian and truly bicultural is even more difficult, requiring twice the effort of being located in any one culture. Add to that a missing father, grinding poverty, and all the usual predatory forces, and it begins to become more clear how tricky it is for individuals like me to get smart enough quickly enough to survive.

Being bicultural can also be twice as rewarding. In spite of some harrowing times on- and off-reservation, I remember well that there was always something pleasurable and comforting associated with the place and people of the Fort Belknap Reservation where I was raised. For many years I did not understand how Gros Ventre values of positive self-identity, family, and community contributed to my sense of well-being. As I became more aware, however, I began to understand that those values compose a belief system equal to any other "religion."

My thinking about how my background relates to teaching has led me to consider that, despite some popular stereotypes, life is not easy for university students either. Even the most pampered individuals encounter the lonesome valley of intellectual challenge, which is probably one of the most level playing fields that exists. In addition to being on their own, a surprising majority of students seem to be working hard to create a better future. As a result, we have much in common, and they seem genuinely interested in American Indian–style solutions to increasingly prevalent problems.

For example, when students realize one of the primary goals of my teaching is to encourage them to get better acquainted with their extended families, it is surprising how many acknowledge the ways their families have been wounded, divided, and separated. When they accept that part of my method includes family-style support systems for learning, they also have a way to understand that rigorous standards do not have to mean just pointing out their academic shortcomings, but can instead mean nurturing and supporting each of them individually. When they decide to trust that I will apply this paradigm, my students become much more open to evaluation and much less concerned with making excuses or complaining.

I have American Indian academic colleagues and nonacademic friends who are cultural nationalists, which means they are oftentimes militant and confrontational. Certainly there is much cause for such activism in the American Indian world, and I am grateful there are those willing to do the necessary work of demanding redress of the theft and cultural genocide committed against American Indians. In fact, their good work allows me to emphasize the things different cultural peoples can have in common, such as family-style support systems in higher education, rather than emphasizing differences. This is an extension of my belief that at the deepest philosophical level all entities have much more in common than previously thought. I am also convinced that it is the collective failure of all world cultures to seek this common ground that has led to the current state of murderous cultural divisions and destruction of the environment. Inescapable evidence of such failure includes a Serb sniper shooting a Muslim mother forced to seek water from a public spigot in Sarajevo; the Amazon rain forest, the lungs of the world, being chopped down to provide temporary grazing for fast-food cattle; and the most recent frenzy of killing in Algeria.

A common thread running through these terrifying events is that all people face the lifelong task of constructing and maintaining an identity. We all go through stages of acquiring basic identity from our families; disconnecting from family to achieve independence; adjusting to early, middle, and late adulthood; and, finally, making the passage we call death. Unfortunately, teaching about these various stages has come to be largely ignored. Although there are treatment industries that have made much progress in dealing with the consequences of our ignorance, they are at best only reactive solutions, and not nearly enough proactive attention is devoted to teaching basic life skills, especially to young people.

When my students discover that positive self-identity, family, and community are primary values of virtually all American Indian cultures, there is an observable resonance on their part. Many belong to the group labeled "Generation X," which has in many ways been indoctrinated to the despair and confusion often articulated as part of the postmodern condition. Many experience feelings of hopelessness at the economic upheaval that has recently been described as "surviving the bottom line," which refers to the way the cost of living keeps rising while economic opportunities keep falling. Others are frightened and confused by violent and destructive world events they interpret as a glimpse of their own future. When these students discover that there are coherent ways of navigating the world they face, and that there are ways of achieving fulfillment and satisfaction without using material wealth and brute force, they are energized.

In the process of privileging capitalism and technology, majority culture has lost ground in dealing with certain crucial issues, such as death and dying. Generally speaking, another countervailing phenomenon found among many traditional Indians is that they often find ways to understand and accept death. Many Indian societies are known as "dream cultures," which teach that by living right, or in a sacred manner, you sleep well; if you sleep well, you dream well. Anyone who has ever dreamed can entertain the idea there are other worlds in addition to our conscious, physical existence. In addition, if you truly believe the earth is your mother, there is much less apprehension about returning to her at the end of physical existence. It is important that we understand what mature cultures teach about death, for the fear of death often leads to the bizarre consequence of mass murder. In order to understand the prevalence of such violence, we must understand how we transform others into sacrificial objects for the ritual unburdening of our own unwanted vices.

Women students are aware they are part of perhaps the largest minority in existence, and they are intrigued by the suggestion that they have much in common with Indians. For example, the recent demonization of white welfare mothers is similar to the portrayal of Indian women as libidinous princesses or unattractive squaws. Once women students acknowledge such similarities, the scope and diversity of their numbers are illuminated. The central place of women in traditional tribal cultures, and the realization of how energetically European males worked to change that role, is a relevant comparison to many of these women's lived experiences. In addition, just as they are delighted to learn of the prevalance of traditional matriarchy, they are also interested in how contemporary Indian women clash and converse with modern feminism.

Another area wherein students consistently seem to relate to Indian worldviews is their observation of the ways Indian people have resisted the process of colonization, because many students now feel they are being subjected to the same process. Although *colonization* is an abstract term used in many confusing ways, certain examples seem to help ground understanding. For instance, Suzy Baer's film *Warrior* tells the story of American Indian political prisoner Leonard Peltier. The setting is Wounded Knee, South Dakota, where the final massacre of plains Indian people took place on December 29, 1890. One scene begins with Peter Matthiessen, author of *In the Spirit of Crazy Horse*, talking about the Wounded Knee confrontation between Indians and the FBI in the summer of 1975, which led to the imprisonment of Peltier. Matthiessen describes how all colonizers attempt to set their victims against one another, usually by providing material advantages to one group while withholding them from another. Baer's film asserts how, in this case, the FBI recruited a Sioux tribal chairman, Dick Wilson, to help support multinational corporations in the acquisition of mineral resources in the Black Hills of South Dakota. Other Sioux resisted Wilson and his followers, resulting in the confrontation at Wounded Knee, a textbook example of the kind of conflict described by Matthiessen.

Bruce Ellison, an attorney working on behalf of Peltier, then points out that the government has told the Indians that, according to the Fort Laramie Treaty of 1868, the Black Hills are theirs; the government has also, however, told white settlers that under the Homestead Acts the Black Hills belong to them. As a result, red and white people were kept busy pointing fingers at one another while multinational corporations, including Union Carbide, Westinghouse, Burlington-Northern, Chevron, Conoco, Exxon, Decker Coal, and Kerr-McGee, made arrangements with whatever willing officials they could find, simply moving in and exploiting resources, a constructive taking of the land by adverse possession.

To understand the stakes involved, consider the following: The Black Hills comprise almost 4 million acres of land. Geologists believe at least half this area contains gold. A gold-mining company in operation at the time of the conflict requested an expansion of eight hundred acres onto "Forest Service land" in the Black Hills. If granted the expansion, the mining company projected an increase in earnings of $3.5 billion. If eight hundred acres is worth $3.5 billion, the worth of 2 million acres illuminates the magnitude of the economics involved, and explains why the FBI, as well as the Pentagon, would become involved in an isolated area of the country where a small group of people were perceived by certain business interests as a threat to their multibillion-dollar operations.[1] The film vividly illustrates how, despite all attempts to explain, disguise,

8

or rationalize the actions, colonization allows empowered groups to take material resources from less powerful "others" by force.

Although it has taken nearly fifty years, I have gradually been able to distance myself from the misleading information that was so much a part of my early life and gravitate toward positive ways of making sense of the complexity of modern existence. Partly out of loyalty to my reservation upbringing—but mainly because I now understand the difference between the manipulative stories presented in education, advertising, and politics and the storytelling that is consistently helpful—I am especially gratified to realize that some of the best information available to deal with the omnipresent social and environmental disasters generates from American Indian worldviews, which, just a short time ago, were thought to be primitive and useless.

One way to more clearly define what helpful information is available from the perceptions of American Indians is to review what is happening in contemporary American Indian education. Evelyn Hu-DeHart, director of ethnic studies at the University of Colorado, has articulated the necessity "to find ample space beyond tokenism for Native American scholarship and discourse."[2] The crucial next step for educational institutions seeking to position themselves for the twenty-first century means a number of things, although that step should not be allowed to become a process of simply making vague allegations of bad faith. Such negative reinforcement creates a "damned if you do, damned if you don't" double bind that is not helpful.

What can be of use is to point out that hiring minimal numbers of faculty from each ethnic group, "papering over" ethnic concerns with task-force kinds of activities that are never acted upon, depending on short-term grant funding for activities that are implemented, and insisting upon maintaining cultural superiority in relations with ethnic groups are all examples of tokenism that can and should be corrected as soon as possible. Of these concerns, maintaining cultural superiority through social integration is perhaps the most complex.

Social integrationists explain that education is a ritual of transition that seeks to blend individuals into educational institutions in preparation for being socialized into adult roles in society. Integrationists also explain that not everyone will become integrated; some students will quit the process. In fact, *most* students from certain ethnic groups quit, leading to Brian Fay's observation that "people are the unwitting victims of processes which cause unnecessary dissatisfaction because they lead people to seek the wrong things and to organize their lives in ways guaranteed to frustrate them."[3] Teachers and students alike get caught up in frustration, which often results from both having become so involved with knowing "who is boss" that teaching and learning are largely put aside.

Although such frustration may have many causes, one of the most difficult to recognize is tension generating from seemingly benevolent authority figures, such as teachers and educational administrators, who are also extensively involved in maintaining power within carefully selected roles. For example, almost everyone will agree that educational institutions have cultural codes that not all individuals or groups will be familiar with. What is less understood is that such codes are often manifestations of power aimed significantly at defining what and how subject matter will be taught and almost always discriminate against less empowered individuals and groups, usually designated "minority." In order to relieve much of the resulting strain, it is necessary to fundamentally transform the present culture of power by bringing it into better balance with the needs of the less powerful.

One way power relations are reinforced is by the insistence that students must first learn "the basics" before they can participate in any higher levels of power themselves: "Summer school programs, learning laboratories, remedial tutors . . . aim to increase minority students' facility to learn essential facts and concepts. . . . the underlying philosophy of this position is that students must grasp hold of the 'culture of power,' by way of learning strategies that enable all students to learn similar facts."[4]

Although learning the basics by memorizing facts and dates provided by an authority figure to large groups of passive students does have a certain utility, it is also an effective tool for the maintenance of cultural superiority. For example, large lecture classes and multiple-choice examinations de-emphasize the individual and control subject matter almost completely. Discussions about abstract values, such as challenging the underlying framework of knowledge and power, do not take place; instead, students are subjected almost exclusively to the "disciplinary" aspect of learning. It is not until the end of the learning process that students sometimes encounter smaller seminars wherein a degree of autonomy exists and they are allowed to participate in dialogic discussions that can become more than just reflections of the point of view of the professor, who in turn may reflect the point of view of the institution, which in turn reflects the point of view of the majority culture.

Large, impersonal classes and severe hierarchical separation between teacher and student have their origins in the Western cultural belief that a single ontological reality, or way of knowing, exists and that there are absolute principles with which all people must agree. In addition, and contrary to some popular beliefs, most college professors labor under workloads that allow little time to inquire about culturally specific pedagogies needed to teach students with diverse cultural backgrounds. Alternative learning strategies do exist, however, and, in the case of American Indians, they can now be observed in the accumulated experience of the tribal-college movement that began with the founding of Navajo Community College in 1968.

Tribal colleges tend to reflect two dramatically different philosophical and pedagogical styles. One style seeks to orient students to the mechanisms of power so that they can transfer to and graduate from mainstream institutions, which is a slightly modified social-integrationist approach. The second style, however, exhibits a radically different conception of knowledge. This vision has the potential to fundamentally transform cultures of power despite the rigid integrationist framework of higher education that demands such things as accreditation requirements and program certification.

It is important to point out that transformation need not mean some kind of reverse discrimination, or overthrow of existing ways of doing things, but can mean, for example, balancing established pedagogy with helpful tribal ways of knowing. One way this can happen is to transform classrooms into communities of learners where there is both individual autonomy and group interaction. Within this conception power becomes less a system of restrictions and more a concept of energy that enables students to find their own voices and histories rather than just taking their turns at learning rules that reinforce unequal relationships.

A common reaction to such transformative ideas is that they may result in mediocre standards and a classroom environment that does not sufficiently emphasize the life skills necessary to compete in the job market. Incorporating different culturally specific ways of knowing, however, need not imply erosion of standards or mean that mainstream academic training needs to be suppressed; rather, working toward a balance of ontological systems that complement one another can be the ultimate goal. One example of better-balanced pedagogy consists of accepting students as co-learners who have much to contribute to the learning process, rather than immediately assuming they know nothing.

Within this paradigm, involvement with learning can also mean that the student-teacher relationship is reformulated so that the authority of the teacher is lessened and the voice of the student increased. As part of the process, large lecture classes and multiple-choice exams are replaced with dialogic learning wherein the teacher is no longer a knowledge expert seeking to exert authority over others. In the words of Paolo Freire: "To consider oneself the proprietor of revolutionary wisdom — which must then be given to (or imposed on) the people — is to retain the old ways. . . . [To be] unable to enter into communion with the people whom are still regarded as totally ignorant, is [to be] grievously self-deceived."[5]

The possibility of linking academic achievement to the concept of social transformation is illustrated by a young English professor who worked with Indian people as part of her duties at a mainstream university. The professor traveled to the reservation as much as possible, interacted with students outside the classroom, and talked with them to implement her knowledge about teaching English. "The teacher was no longer viewed as a knowledge expert, but rather as a co-learner. The learning that took place began with discussions that pertained to the lives of the students."[6]

The teacher succeeded in raising reading levels and enabling Indian students to move into higher level classes, although to do so she found it necessary to reduce the size of classes (she also doubled the number of hours for the classes and tripled the reading and writing assignments). The argument was raised that the classes were too expensive, to which the teacher responded, "I ask them if it's cost efficient . . . to lose students, or if it's efficient to have students who can't read" (104). For universities located in areas where there are significant populations of American Indians, this is an effective example of the tension that immediately arises between efforts to recruit and retain Indian students from tribal and community colleges and resistance to change.

The case study reveals another problem that goes to much harder questions related to achieving true heterogeneity, and is typical of the kinds of things we need to talk about when we talk about tokenism. In the words of the English professor described above: "I haven't had an easy time here. This composition class has been a lightning rod. It makes people unhappy, because it strikes at what they do. Some people think I'm too radical, too young, a woman. They say I've polarized the department. I have moments when I think I'm the luckiest person alive, when I see students clicking, they're getting it. But I wonder if I'm paying too high a price. I'm worried about tenure. The demands on my time are enormous. This class gets me no benefits and has angered some" (104). Her experience is strikingly similar to my own, as well as a dramatic illustration of the consequences of tokenism, where empowered individuals and groups seek both to interact with those who have less power and to maintain strict cultural superiority. Those caught in the middle then encounter the double bind of being made responsible for effective interaction with marginalized students while at the same time encountering serious resistance to change from representatives of the status quo. Combined with heavy teaching loads, ever escalating tenure standards, and dependence upon the goodwill of departments in tenure votes, these kinds of dynamics can easily become overwhelming.

A recent Public Broadcasting System television production titled *Shattering the Silences* addresses many issues facing those now involved in ethnic education.[7] The discussion illuminates the consequences of challenging tradition, which surprisingly often means resolving questions of who will define truth by deciding what will be taught. Within this process, ethnic professors exist in only small numbers, are consistently overburdened and isolated, and daily face the demands of providing new performances that will satisfy both mainstream and minority students, administrators, and colleagues.

In my own experience, the audiences I face every quarter are consistently and thoroughly grounded in either misunderstandings or downright hostile opinions regarding American Indians. Regardless of how interested or curious they might be in me or my work, when it comes time for me to assign grades or when I need to criticize the ways superiors or colleagues interact with ethnic people, both audiences consistently resist. Because both student evaluations and departmental standards are part of the criteria by which my teaching performance is judged, it is absolutely necessary to satisfy both parties without appearing disingenuous. Failure to do so puts tenure at risk, which is the same thing as risking being fired.

So far I have been able to deal with this double bind in interaction with students by balancing my pedagogy carefully between the oral tradition of American Indians and the European written tradition, with strong emphasis on students relating their own lives to the materials. In practice this means that as soon as students realize they will be asked to respond as individuals, rather than as part of a large group, they cease to rely on cultural knowledge they have acquired elsewhere and begin to gather new information. By relating as individuals, and by gathering new information, students are able to free themselves from stereotypes about Indians and from the power structures they have been conditioned to expect in their educational experiences.

Interaction with superiors and colleagues is considerably more difficult. Even in the most benign situations I have been unable to accomplish more than the most superficial changes in existing departmental infrastructures. Institutions with which I have interacted have consistently been interested in "opening up areas of study," but they have also been adamant in defining "opening up" as not including anything but the most facile criticism of mainstream styles and as hiring no more than the barest minimum numbers of ethnic faculty.

This sketch of how I deal with some of the most complex aspects of intercultural relations provides only a glimpse of what it takes to survive as an ethnic professor, and has taken years to develop. Developing such methodology is so difficult because few if any precedents exist, and, in the absence of any effective models, the process becomes one of trial and error, with severe penalties awaiting missteps. The burnout of ethnic educators discussed in *Shattering the Silences* becomes more understandable when one considers the usual situation of near complete cultural and personal isolation; the fine line that exists between educating and alienating students, colleagues, and administrators; and the low pay and staggering workload that affects personal relationships.

Although these obstacles are formidable, they must be endured in order to effect changes such as creating climates for learning that include cultural knowledge embedded in stories, songs, and prayer, as well as skills and facts. A way to begin is by giving systemwide accrediting and legitimizing forces more flexibility so that they may not only synthesize measures of assessment and accountability, but also configure alternative ways of interacting with foundationally different knowledge systems, such as tribal colleges that emphasize tribal worldviews.

In *Tribal Colleges*, a report published by the Carnegie Foundation, Paul Boyer summarizes the threshold problem faced by Indian communities attempting higher education: "At almost all of the institutions, salaries are far too low, libraries are shockingly underfunded, and administrators struggle to operate with day-to-day budget constraints that other higher learning institutions would totally reject. Although a few of the colleges have accommodating campuses, many are getting by with mismatched trailers or unsuitable buildings converted from other uses."[8] As with many things related to the complexity of ethnic peoples, however, these facts only touch the surface.

A larger problem, related to the maintenance of cultural superiority over Indians, is found in the ways elementary and secondary education has been facilitated by simply transferring control, funding, personnel, and facilities from the Bureau of Indian Affairs to tribes under the auspices of the Indian Self-Determination Act. Higher education, however, tends to open up possibilities beyond teaching "the basics," which is interpreted as fostering possible threats to existing power structures and is not encouraged. Because the power structures are unwilling to advance beyond disciplinary learning, tribal leaders have been faced with undertaking higher education almost entirely on their own.

There have been many interesting results of relying on the initiatives of tribal leaders, including concerns that are typical of the harder questions related to contemporary social evolution: "What does it mean to be a tribal college? Is a tribal community college an institution like any other community college, except that it is governed and staffed by tribal members? In a country that espouses pluralism and integration among the races, is an institution that segregates itself by race a paradox? What are the implications for the structure and pedagogy of an institution that calls itself *tribal*? Or are there no implications?"[9]

Despite the absence of any role models, as well as the added pressure of the requirements of accrediting agencies, tribal colleges have managed to construct themselves so that they are not merely colleges that happen to serve Indians; rather, they are Indian colleges in structure and pedagogy. Part of what it means to be a tribal college is reflected in the words of a tribal member who has been president of a tribal college for eight years: "Our value system is represented in the college structure in many forms. Student activities frequently have a family focus. Elder clansmen and clanswomen are integrally involved in moments of achievement. Consensus building is a consistent means of decision making. Forgiveness is employed in grading and withdrawal. Students are encouraged to learn in cooperative groups. Individual student enrollment is accepted by college staff as a family function, counseling and retention strategies are designed in that light" (127). Such information offers a glimpse of how tribal colleges may contribute to mainstream ways of doing things. For example, tribal cultures have always worked to include as many individuals as possible in meaningful activities, as opposed to limiting such activities to a few organizational leaders. Meaningful involvement contributes to rituals of empowerment rather than integration, and enables students to draw on their own histories and voices; this in turn can gradually become an educational process of creating productive conflict, rather than enforcing a unifying discourse that inevitably excludes those on the margins.

Productive conflict can also invite interrogation of such things as academic support centers, student orientation, and summer programs in ways that point out how those activities often create the perception that Indian students are less adept than others. One way to counter this is to consider how the usual annual Pow-wow, the Native American student union, and small numbers of ethnic faculty can be expanded to include a wider range of teachers, cultural activities, symbols, and events that speak to true heterogeneity rather than outdated multiculturalism. For example, in the Oregon higher education system, which is located in the heart of rich and diverse Indian cultures, interaction with those cultures is painfully limited and forced to be on a par with the other major color groups, all of which have much less history in the region.

Lakota historian and cultural critic Vine Deloria Jr. says: "Perhaps we should suspect the real motives of the academic community. They have the Indian field well defined and under control. Their concern is not the ultimate policy that will affect the Indian people, but merely the creation of new slogans and doctrines by which they can climb the university totem pole." [10] Indeed, values of positive self-identity, family, community, and environment are all expressions of American Indian philosophy that persist in living Indian communities and can be observed in stories and texts generating from American Indian literature and other sources. What is much less apparent are the circumstances as well as the cost of preserving such values, in terms both of historic loss and continuing struggle.

The persecution of Indians has decreased as the process of colonization has become more complete, but only after some 98 percent of the original inhabitants of this country were slaughtered. And, although persecution has slowed, it has not, by any stretch of the imagination, stopped altogether. In fact, Indian people still live under a policy of continuing genocide enforced by the American government and tolerated by the American people.

In part because of their unfortunate circumstances, and in part due to certain failures to live up to their own responsibilities, Indian people live with internal oppression as well as external oppression by the majority culture. Internal oppression takes the form of Indian opportunism associated with carrying out the policies of the American government against fellow Indians, exclusivist territoriality manifested by Indian people excluding, attacking, or ignoring fellow Indians in many ways, and various forms of domestic abuse perpetrated by Indian people on community members, family members, and themselves.

Because it is by storytelling that Indian people have always survived, it is necessary to tell these unattractive stories as well as those of a more positive nature. In fact, it can be shown that stories of suffering and deprivation serve a useful purpose in terms of properly contextualizing the past so that it not only allows Indian people to endure the present, but also allows them to imagine the present as the past of a better-imagined future.

A way to start this story is by acknowledging that American Indian people have recently experienced the end of the world. It is ironic that Indians are so strongly associated with horses, for it has been their lot to "Behold a pale horse: and his name that sat on him was Death, and Hell followed with him (Rev. 68). They are postapocalypse people who, as such, have tremendous experience to offer all other people who must, in their own time, experience their own cultural death as part of the natural cycle. The ways in which American Indian people have suffered, survived, and managed to go on, communicated through storytelling, have tremendous potential to affect the future of all mankind.

The process by which this information might be organized is temporal unification of the past and future with the present. While there is much useful information to be gleaned from the past, there is also much that must simply be forgotten. All people, Indian and others alike, must find a way to imagine a better future, or the earth's environmental resources will soon be depleted. If proper consideration of the past can be linked to rational planning for the future, much of what needs to be done now is made obvious.

It is at this juncture that negative capability can be of use. Modern cultures have never come to grips with certain concepts (such as the fear of death), which contributes to our present inertia. If we can learn to say the unspeakable, to talk of the seemingly unknowable, we will be able to face our fears and move beyond lying, avoidance, scapegoating, and hoarding of wealth as the means of comforting ourselves.

If each individual can discover ways to achieve self-efficacy, or find meaning throughout the stages of life, we can once again turn our energies to what the Indians for thousands of years called the Good Road. The study of American Indian literature is an excellent vehicle for investigation of these issues. In part, this is a reflection of the fact that what has matured within American Indian literature is an undeniable facility with the techniques and tropes of modernism, as well as a profound awareness of conflicting epistemologies. I believe this kind of pluralism, as the foundation of a clearly defined vision, is the best means of approaching the complexity of our multicultural world.

A wide variety of American writings, as well as certain aspects of Canadian, European, and world literatures, are relevant. For example, moving freely among genres and disciplines has produced courses of study such as American Indians in Law, Literature, and Social Sciences. Another example is finding connections between such diverse scholars as American Indian historian Vine Deloria Jr. and Canadian-European theorist Northrop Frye. Both suggest that at the deepest philosophical level our universe must have as a structure a set of relationships in which all entities participate. Deloria's sense is that within the physical world this universal structure can best be understood as a recognition of the sacredness of places. Frye, on the other hand, recognizes the unique nature of religious symbolism, its apparent correspondence with places, its vibrant ability to reassert itself in times of spiritual crisis, and the implications of the existence or absence of a universal symbol system of religious experience.

There is much to be learned through a careful tracing, along those paths not already guarded by intellectual gatekeepers, of the border lines where comparative experiences meet and separate. Perhaps, for example, the conflicts of competing religions over land have led to much of our social, political, and military conflicts among people. I believe strongly that Keatsian negative capability, the unification of past/present/future, and principles of self-efficacy, from what I have termed post-apocalypse theory, are helpful means of addressing the kinds of pressing social and environmental problems facing world cultures today.

Because we seem to have such difficulty utilizing the past, and because we seem so powerless to plan for the future, especially in terms of environmental resources, it is imperative to investigate sincerely all means of discovering usable pasts and a better-imagined future. Although it is appropriate to emphasize American Indian sources, it is also important to add the balance of strong comparative and multidisciplinary orientations. This conception aspires not only to function as a leading edge of both written and spoken theories, but also to forge connections with the living communities upon which academic work is based.

# House Made of Cards
## *The Construction*
## *of American Indians*

THE DESTRUCTION OF AMERICAN INDIANS BY European diseases and military technology is obvious. What is less visible is how various language appellations have harmed Indian cultures. For example, words such as *savage, enemy, them,* and *other* create the objectification necessary for one group to treat another as if the members were not fellow human beings.

Once intellectual separation is achieved, the ways and means of destruction become of primary concern; rationalization follows. Justification of the destruction of American Indians has been so successful that contemporary majority culture has effectively suppressed acknowledgment of wrongs and ignores continuing genocide.

Such denial can be observed in many ways. For example, when I first began to introduce into the classroom materials illuminating American Indian genocide, the reaction was always the same. A small but passionate number of students would insist on acknowledging the horror of what had happened, but the majority regularly asserted they were not responsible because the atrocities had happened before they were born. Pointing out the continuing genocide among Indian people, as evidenced by the forty-seven-year average life expectancy for Indian males, was a way to counterargue the claim, but such point-by-point argument was never truly effective.

What I find more productive is to ask students to prepare an individual oral performance in which they relate their own lives to the classroom discussions and readings. The shift to individuality successfully redefines certain group dynamics. For example, when students were treated as part of a large group they relied on information they had already acquired from family, friends, and the media. Conversely, when they are invited to examine their own experiences and relate them to those of American Indians, the students look more closely at the ways tribal people lived in the past, their present circumstances, and what their ways of life have to offer for the future.

I also ask students to write a paper relating what they know about American Indians and explaining where they obtained the information. It is amazing not only to realize how much nearly all students know about Indians, but also to note their wide variety of sources. Unfortunately, most of the cultural information students have absorbed at random is not very useful, ranging from urban myths, to stereotypes, to the Hollywood paradigm of the eighteenth-century Sioux warrior. Although these images are not particularly useful, they are not nearly as pernicious as the other kinds of troublesome information that form the basis of the formal and informal codes by which Indian people are dealt with by the forces of government, law, education, publishing, and art. These more formal sources of information first gave authority to the idea that Indians were uncivilized, and now depict them as inherently maladjusted.

In "The Man Made of Words," his masterful discussion of the relation between language and experience, Kiowa writer N. Scott Momaday says, "The greatest tragedy that can befall us is to go unimagined."[1] As with many things related to American Indian cultures, the more important meanings of this statement are found in its deeper, postmodern allegorical subtleties. "The Man Made of Words," written around 1970, intensified the issues among language, landscape, and identity to show them as much more complex than simply a reflection of those places where we live or upon which we make money. In fact, Momaday's insights are much clearer to us now, when we are coming to realize that all relationships, animate and inanimate, are complexly intertwined.

Similarly, Momaday's observation of the tragic nature of "going unimagined" not only relates to events and characters, but also is connected to the very structure of ideas that events and characters are intended to convey.

Momaday's statement has an unusual complexity because Indians have never suffered from being unimagined. In fact, D. H. Lawrence noted a sincere yearning on the part of many Americans to *be* Indian. On a less romantic level, Louis Owens observes, "In fact, the Indian in today's world consciousness is a product of literature, history, and art, and a product that, as an invention, often bears little resemblance to actual, living Native American people."[2] These inventions, or imaginings, including the stereotypes of noble savage, stoic warrior, libidinous princess, cigar-store totem, rainmaking shaman, and tearful ecologist, had many social uses. Some have framed elaborate rationalizations for widespread abuses of people, animals, and the environment, while others have served the marketplace, most noticeably in advertising. Further, it has been said of the cultural imaginings written into law that "Our 'fine-feathered friends' [Indians] serve as the miner's canary of Western cultural devastation, as Felix Cohen noted forty years ago in the *Handbook of Federal Indian Law*. If they go, so do we."[3]

Imagining Indians as links to a usable past entails seeing them as harbingers of the future. Such ongoing, and very common, mental gymnastics lead us back to the postmodern allegorical structure implied in Momaday's concern about being unimagined. There is a Keatsian negative capability in all the stereotypes from which American Indians have suffered, for even at their worst the stereotypes are evidence of deep and abiding interest. Lionel Trilling, in *The Opposing Self: Nine Essays in Criticism*, says, "Negative Capability, the faculty of not having to make up one's mind about everything, depends upon the sense of one's personal identity and is the sign of personal identity. Only the self that is certain of its existence, of its identity, can do without the armor of systematic certainties."[4] This relation of negative capability to intelligent choice is crucial to understanding postapocalypse American Indians.

Trilling also believed that it is the very essence of intelligence to recognize irresolvable complexity. If the failure of Indian people to assimilate to mainstream culture can be perceived as a set of complex and intelligent choices, rather than as a state of being helpless or childlike, many assumptions may prove to be circumstantial, if not incorrect. This might be understood in a number of ways, one of which is considering the possibility that the stereotype of Indians as helpless children is actually a projection of a condition of mainstream culture onto others. If this is the case, it further illuminates the reasons American Indians have been so slow to "acculturate," preferring instead to wait until such a projection collapses of its own weight.

The results of this long wait have begun to appear, as mainstream culture increasingly looks to tribal worldviews for ways to deal with escalating social and environmental problems. In fact, the people of Joseph, Oregon, located in a beautiful mountain valley that was taken from the Nez Perce, "want the Indians to return and are even assembling the financing to buy a large patch of real estate for them. They regard the return of the Nez Perce as a way to help replace the dying logging and ranching economy that was created as a justification for removing the Indians in the first place."[5]

It is also easy to see the problems of being imagined improperly, as in the case of stereotypes. Less easy to grasp is any inverse value in the ways Indians have been excessively or improperly imagined. However, it is in this negative capability that some important seeds of recovery and regeneration for Indian peoples first begin to germinate. Perhaps the most significant example can be found in American Indian literature. Within this writing is found some of Indian peoples' best hope for recovery of identity, redescription of stereotypes, and resistance to further colonization. As a creative process, such writing is often postmodern in the sense that various seemingly established literary forms frequently give way to their opposites; for example, the typical "hero" may give way to other kinds of imaginings such as the antihero, and the seeming villain may be redeemed.

The many ways in which American Indians have been imagined by the mainstream have been thoroughly documented.[6] For example, Robert F. Berkhofer Jr. in *The White Man's Indian* covers topics such as "the Idea of the Indian," "the Scientific Image of the Indian," "Imagery [of Indians] in Literature, Art, and Philosophy," and "Imagery [of Indians] and White Policy."[7] Mainstream literary criticism since the late

1970s has increasingly examined a wide variety of materials produced by Indian writers.[8] For example, Andrew Wiget's *Native American Literature*, published in 1985, discusses Oral Narrative, Oratory and Oral Poetry, The Beginnings of a Written Literature, Modern Fiction, and Contemporary Poetry. In 1990, in a bibliographic text, A. LaVonne Brown Ruoff added sources to each of Wiget's basic categories and included sources for new categories, such as Life History and Autobiography, Teaching American Indian Literatures, Women's Studies, Films and Journals, and American Indian Journals.[9]

Less discussed are American Indians' ideas of themselves and how such intellectual sovereignty affects their relation to a contemporary society driven more and more by market forces and characterized by disturbing social, racial, and economic inequities. Unfettered capitalism, where market forces determine the social good, is causing a "gangsterization" of culture in which corruption and greed dominate, unchecked by either weakened public institutions or individual leadership. The problem of race in American society quickly leads to a dialogue about other abuses of power, ranging from the domination of women by men to discrimination against gays and other minorities. Although these examples of mainstream ideology are predominant, Indian authors often exploit their negative capability, viewing them as opportunities as well as liabilities. Traditional Indian structures of language, story, and humor allow American Indians to use such opportunities to develop new literatures and criticism.

One such opportunity exists in the academic world, in response to which Lakota and UCLA American Indian Studies Center scholar Kenneth Lincoln says in his 1983 book, *Native American Renaissance*, "My literary colleagues have given me a disciplined home from which to stray, and I am appreciative."[10] Lincoln establishes the tone for his work in his introduction to Louise Erdrich's newly republished *Love Medicine*: "There is little, if any, old-style ethnography in the fiction. . . . Daily survival precedes cultural purism. What does not come with the terrain and times must tend to itself" (xv). *Native American Renaissance* is a considerable departure from the mainstream conceptual world that, nonetheless, melds that world with ideas derived from Indian worldviews. In the process, Lincoln makes considerable progress toward addressing a central question—whether the literatures "carry the power to move us" (10).

Even more recently, American Indian scholars Louis Owens and Robert Warrior have continued to advance scholarship by and about Indians. Owens, in *Other Destinies: Understanding the American Indian Novel*, has clarified and expanded interpretation of the major texts of the Native American Renaissance. Warrior, in *Tribal Secrets: Recovering American Indian Intellectual Traditions*, has produced work "that explores the extent to which, after more than two centuries of impressive literary and critical production, critical interpretation of those writings can proceed primarily from Indian sources."[11]

Despite all this good and necessary work, urgent questions still beg critical response. Barre Toelken asks: What is "Indian," specifically, about Indian writings? What is "seeing from a native eye?" And, to rephrase Toelken's Navajo informant, Henry Yellowman, "How many kinds of words will it hold?"[12] How can important theoretical frameworks articulated by mainstream academics such as Arnold Krupat and Karl Kroeber be linked to actual indigenous experience? How does the work of American Indian writers respond to the urgent theoretical questions raised in the scholarship about American Indians?

The foundation upon which to discuss these questions is the complex issue of identity. "For the contemporary Indian novelist—in every case a mixedblood who must come to terms in one form or another with peripherality as well as both European and Indian ethnicity—identity is the central issue and theme, and, as [James] Clifford has suggested, ethnic identity is always 'mixed, relational, and inventive.'"[13] Examples include the unique ways in which, as part of the ongoing evolution of Indian identity, American Indian autobiographical writings have emerged, and the ways they differ from both creative writing and scholarship. Such writings include Black Hawk's early telling of his story with the help of a Euramerican, Charles Eastman's stand-alone autobiography, and N. Scott Momaday's combination of autobiographical facts with works of art. In fact, the autobiographical form has proved congenial to a growing number of Indians interested in constituting and preserving self through writing.

Our need to establish intellectual sovereignty by these means and more is made clear by an existing body of work tending largely to suppress the voices of Indians themselves. Review of these older ideas is helpful in considering the contemporary authenticity debate. We need to redefine past debates to make them more useful for our consideration of the future. For example, in the past Indian people were typically called natives, Native Americans, American Indians, aboriginal people, Indians, original inhabitants, and tribal people, among other names. Both the continued existence of all these terms and the denial of virtually all of them by Indians themselves in one situation or another reflect the complexity of Indian identity.

The Indian people I know call themselves "Induns," or "Indi'n," about which Kenneth Lincoln says:

The word "Indi'n," with its dialectical elision, crosses the first boundary between native tribal peoples and immigrant Euroamericans. America is not India, we all know by now, and these tribal aborigines are nominally not In-*di*-ans. They do not spell or speak themselves as such; by inverse relation to "proper" English, indeed, they collate dialectically across a continent as differing peoples with hundreds of cultural tongues. "Since dialect, at least to the oppressor, is part and parcel of the negative stereotype," John Lowe notes, "pride in dialect constitutes inversion, transforming an oppressive signifier of otherness into a pride-inspiring prism, one which may be used for the critical inspection of 'the other.'"[14]

Although Indian people call themselves "Induns," "Indi'ns," "Skins," or "Grovons," the terms are separatist twists on old misnomers, taken in and inverted in ways that lie at the heart of Indian humor and resistance. The failure of these insider terms to penetrate the mainstream bespeaks the complexity of Indian humor, and, perhaps, the sting of its rebuke.

This complexity is joined to emotional and political intensity. Thus, discussions about identity escalate almost immediately to related controversies, such as whether "outsiders" should have access to Indian literature, with energetic arguments offered up on both sides. Some minority writers argue that grassroots-type Indian experience is important to the creation and appreciation of the literature, while some majority writers see an insistence on this kind of experience as ethnic essential-ism directed against them.

Jack Forbes, in his essay "Colonialism and Native American Liter-ature: Analysis," offers the minority (Indian) point of view. In discussing his definition of Indian literature, Forbes states, "Native American lit-erature must consist in works produced by persons of Native identity and/or culture. . . ." Arnold Krupat responds as an academic from a ma-jority point of view in his book *The Voice in the Margin*: "it is the oral and periodical literature that is for him [Forbes] the only discourse be-ing produced today that may appropriately be called *Indian* literature because these alone are primarily for an Indian audience by authors whose primary self-identification is Indian, working in forms historically evolved by or at least currently most readily accessible to that primary audience."[15]

The interchange between Forbes and Krupat represents a typical current intellectual conflict. First, both sides represent some need to define, or "name," the other by employing strategies of writing and rep-resentation. Second, there is some truth on both sides — both are au-thoritative with respect to different systems. Yet, both views are flawed when presented as absolute principles. The "Indian" perspective has the potential to exclude those members of a group whose place is validated by blood heritage but whose life experience lies largely outside the "nor-mal" experience of the group, as in the case of urban Indians. On the other hand, the "white" viewpoint fails to recognize the value of having actually lived in an Indian community on a day-to-day basis as a means of possessing a fuller understanding of a particular culture. In both po-sitions, persons who are known and recognized *in Indian communities* remain seriously underrepresented, especially in terms of the study and dissemination of Indian literature.

The Forbes-Krupat debate is a microcosm of the Indian-white social universe, where two different worldviews clash over potentially valuable territory. To see this type of conflict as generative rather than reductive is tricky. As with recognizing many things related to "the other," however, it is important to accept the potential for negative capa-bility. Such acceptance not only enables the relation of negative capability to intelligent choice, but also allows us to to see how contention can produce valuable new ideas rather than just destructive behavior.

Territories and their boundaries are often conceptualized by names and naming, which is in turn important to the process of constructing identity. An example is the tribe known as Falls Indians, Atsina, White Clay People, Chalk Men, Gros Ventres (say Grovons), Northern Arapaho, and, finally, the People of Many Names. All the names have a touch of contradiction about them, often failing to make sense when juxtaposed with terms such as *full-blood*, *mixed-blood*, *tribal person*, *urban Indian*, *Pan-Indian*, and the like. Ultimately, however, names such as these often create tension between signifier and signified.

For instance, let's consider the Falls Indians, who have come to be known by the unflattering term *Gros Ventre*, which means "big belly." This misnomer comes from misinterpretation of the motion of hands outward from the abdomen, signifying "people who live by the waterfalls" in sign language. Being named from *without*, regardless of flattering or unflattering context, creates tension because of the importance of naming; to name something is to give it its place in the world. For members of a minority culture to be named "big belly" by members of the dominant culture, as the Falls Indians were named by French voyageurs, represents a significant loss of power. Hanay Geiogamah unmasks certain psychic forces related to naming in his satiric play *Foghorn*, in which the Lone Ranger calls Tonto his "faithful Injun companion" once too often and gets his throat cut.[16]

Examining some names given to Indian people helps "unpack" them so they may be seen more clearly. To begin, the current signifier of choice for people of Native American background is *Indian*, with some situational variants. It is common knowledge that the word *Indian* is an invention of people of European origin, an extension of the term originally coined by Christopher Columbus. What is not as commonly known is that considerable time passed before the term acquired a standardized usage among Europeans. In fact, "Centuries passed before many of the politically, culturally, and linguistically separate peoples native to North America willingly accepted and used the word *Indian* as a meaningful appellation for themselves. . . . Even today, there are many

Hopi, Tlingit, Menomini and others who resent being labeled in this manner."[17]

Other terms such as *half-breed, mixed-blood, Métis,* and *brûle* were coined by the English and French colonists. These terms, a product of European preoccupation with racial classification, eventually became part of the cultural vocabulary of North Americans. Such names were then "fleshed out" with visual and verbal images, and, prompted by governmental policy, early American writers wrote romances filled with images of "the Indian" as an inhuman savage with a taste for the blood of white women and children.

The foundation for these kinds of portrayals lies deep in European notions of racial categorization, as James Clifton observes: "The classification and treatment of people by race presumes that they share inherent, intrinsic, inescapable characteristics. They are of a race automatically at birth, in the American idiom *by blood,* and this is a status they cannot escape by their achievements, accomplishments, or any form of mobility" (ibid., 26). Such pigeonholing establishes boundaries between groups by classifying individuals according to the colors white, black, red, and yellow. This stratification becomes problematic when the concept of *race* is thought unequivocally to determine the behavior and characteristics of a group or individual. The assumption that actions are controlled from without rather than being the products of free will functions as a kind of Pandora's box; once opened, the justifications for all kinds of oppression are loosed.

Clifton makes the further observation that "Originally, no native North American society subscribed to the idea of biological determination of identity or behavior" (11). Thus, he contends that, rather than skin color, Indians were interested in such distinctions as language and other practical skills, family relationships, social facility, and loyalty. In spite of such helpful observations, however, Clifton falls into a common trap among those who have sought to understand the dynamics of race: he does not move beyond basic conclusions to reach a level of critical thinking that might effect positive change.

For example, in the context of history, Indians were quite conscious of who belonged to what groups, especially those considered "enemies," an "us against them" perception. Today, most Indians are trapped between their older ideas of group identity and standard Euramerican principles. These Euramerican principles of assigning group and individual identity, deeply rooted in bureaucracy, are determined by blood, even though it is known that race does not inherently determine the identities and characteristics of individuals and groups, that there is no chemical analysis for "Indian blood," and that the determinations of blood quantum that do exist were originally made almost whimsically, as a result of political and economic circumstance.

This bureaucratic system of assigning racial or ethnic identity has evolved into a practice of inclusion-exclusion based on strategies of writing and representation. In many instances, whites have employed their earlier access to written tradition to exclude Indians by defining them as alien to white standards. As Robert Berkhofer has written in *The White Man's Indian*, "whites perceived, observed, evaluated, and interpreted Indians as literary and artistic images."[18]

Whites also interpret Indians as objects of legal policy, and arbitrary legal constructs are widespread in Indian-populated areas. The United States limits legal recognition and access to federal services to people who can document at least one-fourth Indian blood or, in some limited cases, to those who are known and recognized by existing Indian communities. Similarly, in Canada there is a distinction made between *status* and *nonstatus* Indians. Status Indians are legally recognized by the government and have all the attendant rights and privileges. Nonstatus Indians are apparently still considered Indian, but are not entitled to benefits.

The almost ridiculous lengths to which legal constructs are carried in attempting to define Indians can be illustrated by the efforts of the U.S. federal government. The power to define a *tribe* legally (but not socially, politically, or anthropologically) resides solely with the federal government. The power to define what it is to be an *individual* Indian or tribal member resides in part with the federal government, but there is also substantial tribal authority to define individual membership. At the same time, the tribes have inherited the blood-quantum legacy and, for practical purposes, have not been able to move beyond it. All these elements contribute to an extremely complex conception of identity.

One illustration of the complexity of defining the American Indian is the bylaws of the National Indian Education Association (NIE), which state: "For purposes of the NIE Constitution the term American Indian shall mean any person who: (1) is a member of a tribe, band, or other organized group of Indians, including those tribes, bands, or groups terminated since 1940 and those recognized now or in the future by the state in which they reside, or who is a descendant, in the first or second degree, of any such member, or (2) is considered by the Secretary of the Interior to be an Indian for any purpose, (3) is an Eskimo or Aleut or other Alaska Native, or (4) is recognized as an Indian by his community" (Membership, art. 3). In addition, the *Federal Register* contains seven mandatory criteria for federal acknowledgment. The first section demands evidence establishing that the petitioner has been historically and continuously identified as an American Indian entity. The section then presents seven additional subsections establishing various kinds of allowable evidence.[19]

These kinds of criteria resemble legal statutes, presenting standards generated from history, relationships, and property that individuals and tribes must meet to "make their case" to the federal government that they qualify as Indians. Nevertheless, it does not appear that the criteria advance understanding of the elements and boundaries of Indian culture as much as they exercise an authority to define Indian identity.

The criteria do make it clear, however, that Indian people are a minority defined by the majority culture. It is a definition that diverges widely in most instances from their own kinship and place-oriented notions of themselves. A related question that arises is how tribes identify their own people at the present time, and whether their methodology of identification is contaminated by majority domination. At the community level it seems that clan or family identification happens much as it did in the days before contact with whites. At the governmental level, however, Bureau of Indian Affairs (BIA) regulations have interfered with the identification process so that the system is now politically oriented, highly artificial, and divisive. Thus, both Indians and the BIA actively campaign to shrink Indian numbers, further illustrating how exclusion is a vital component of interaction from both directions.

African American scholar Houston Baker looks at this structuring from his perspective in *"Race," Writing, and Difference*. Baker emphasizes that certain "scientific" notions are mistaken: "Biology, anthropology, and the human sciences in general all believed, in former times, that there was such a phenomenon as 'race.' Current genetic research demonstrates that there is no such thing." In the same work, Henry Louis Gates Jr. suggests that race is not a matter of blood or genetics, but is cultural. Speaking of black literature, he says, "There is no question that representations of black character-types in European and American literature have a history — and a life — of their own, generating repetitions, revisions, and refutations. Within African and Afro-American literature, there can be no question that the *texts* that comprise these traditions repeat, refute, and revise key, canonical tropes and topoi peculiar to those *literary* traditions."[20]

In addition to the mistaken notion that identity is a matter of blood, other factors have created pressure in recent years to supplant the Indian-blood requirement with a system that legitimates those individuals known and recognized as part of existing Indian communities. One of these factors is intermarriage between "enrolled" or "status" Indians and others.

The increasing popularity of claiming to be an "Indian" creates another challenge for cultural definitions of identity: "every time the value of being Indian increases, the number of persons of marginal or ambiguous ancestry who claim to be Indians increases."[21] The reference is in part to a series of economic "opportunities" created by the federal government, beginning with the Indian Trade and Intercourse Act of 1834, which established preferential hiring for persons of Indian blood within the Indian Service, or BIA. Later, the General Allotment/Dawes Act of 1887 awarded "legal title" to land to people successfully claiming Indian status. More recently, the Indian Claims Commission Act of 1946 and a number of aid programs established during the 1960s have encouraged individuals to assert Indian identity.

The complexity of contemporary Indian identity is thus derived from all these elements. The results are often bizarre: "In truth, many contemporary status Indians . . . have no native American biological ancestry at all. Conversely, there are millions of Americans who have much native biological ancestry, such as Mexican-Americans, but they are not classed or treated as Indians" (ibid., 23). On the other hand, "Underlying this culturally patterned system of assigning individual and group identity by race is a simple, implicit principle: any degree of . . . Indian blood overrides an individual's or a group's other antecedents and fixes racial identity" (12). Whether individuals or groups today are accepted as "legal" Indians is determined essentially by political decisions, and "Such decisions are political because they invariably involve access to resources" (23).

A recent example of politicization of identity can be found in the April 29, 1992, issue of the *Chronicle of Higher Education*. In an article titled "Claims of American-Indian Heritage Become Issue for Colleges Seeking to Diversify Enrollments," ways of excluding students who claim Indian heritage are discussed. Indian educators at the University of Michigan articulated their support of tribal affiliation and blood-quantum "proof" as requirements for being recognized as Indian. An opposing viewpoint, ironically advanced by the non-Indian director of admissions, pointed out that tribal affiliation is unfair to urban Indians who "may develop an affiliation and a better understanding of their heritage through programs at the university" (A30).

It should be enough that students who consider themselves Indians and are known and recognized in existing Indian communities, rural or urban, be accepted as such, as is apparently Michigan's policy. "Known and recognized" is the key concept and refers to unconditional acceptance of those individuals acculturated in Indian communities since childhood; in addition, acceptance of those who are living or have lived within Indian culture for a significant period of time is granted on a case-by-case basis. Within these boundaries, asking how to exclude individuals from Indian culture is clearly a way to reduce the number of Indians compared with asking how to include them.

The stakes involved with identity are illustrated most dramatically in relationship to benefits. Receipt of claim money and federal funds from the 1960s through the 1980s depended on one's enrollment as a member of the tribe and of the community, echoing the enrollment debacle during the Osage oil boom discussed in Terry Wilson's *Underground Reservation*. Oil wealth was very divisive to the Osages, as people struggled to enroll themselves or their children or grandchildren, often by gaining approval from the treaty committee or business council to change blood degree. The new money brought the blood-quantum system to the fore and highlighted it in ways that continue to figure importantly in political interaction. For example, even today cultural identity can be changed or reclaimed in part by a change of blood degree "on paper."

Part of the difficulty in understanding Indian identity comes from the process by which it was first destroyed by European colonizers, then reconstructed in ways that served the colonizers' purposes. Deeply embedded in the process are issues of racism, adaptation, and self-realization, all obscured by the desire of Indians to find some kind of order in the complexity of human acts, and of whites to rationalize various actions. Despite such difficulty, all surviving groups of Indians have made strategic accommodations with external forms of government. They have survived acute demographic and cultural crises, as well as periods of change and revival. They have found means to revive and invent lives as Indians in the twentieth century as part of an ongoing process, politically contested and historically unfinished.[22]

Nevertheless, among contemporary Indian people issues of identity continue to cause a painful polarity that is also suffused with negative capability. Joy Harjo, a contemporary writer, says of her own mixed parentage: "Well, it means trouble . . . [but] . . . I realize in a way that you have to believe that you're special to be born like that because why would anybody give you such a hard burden . . . unless they knew you could come through with it, unless with it came some special kind of vision to help you get through it all and to help others through it. . . ."[23]

In *The Predicament of Culture*, James Clifford asks a number of related questions: "Who has the authority to speak for a group's identity or authenticity? What are the essential elements and boundaries of a culture? How do self and other clash and converse in the encounters of ethnography, travel, modern interethnic relations? What narratives of development, loss, and innovation can account for the present range of local oppositional movements?"[24]

In response to the first question, the federal government and the legal system have largely assumed the authority to speak for Indian identity/authenticity. An incident involving contemporary artist and activist Jimmie Durham helps demonstrate how Indian identity is thus restricted. Durham was founding director of the International Indian Treaty Council of the American Indian Movement and is currently editor of the newspaper *Art and Artists*. The August/September 1991 issue of *Art-Talk* magazine, in a column titled "Lack of Indian Credentials Cancels Show," reported:

Concerned with Jimmie Durham's "inability to document his Cherokee heritage," the American Indian Contemporary Arts Gallery in San Francisco called off a one-man show for him which had been scheduled for July 12–August 31. This decision was made, according to the gallery, in order to be in compliance with Public Law 101-644, "The Indian Arts and Crafts Act of 1990." PL 101-644 provides "very stringent and precise definitions" of Indian art and Indian artists, and imposes "very stiff fines and penalties for willful misrepresentation." The Indian Arts and Crafts Board of the Department of Interior is charged with implementation of the law, and alleged violations are referred to the F.B.I. . . . (17)

The seriousness with which the notion of who is and who is not "Indian" has come to be regarded within and without Indian country is aptly illustrated by its intrusion into the art world. In this instance it seems clear that the Euramerican legal system speaks for Indians with regard to whom they should consider authentic. Furthermore, that authenticity is based on blood quantum, which makes it questionable at best.

The essential elements and boundaries of culture here seem to be economic, with "very stiff fines and penalties imposed for willful misrepresentation" of Indianness. Jimmie Durham's clash with the federal government becomes an instance of an "other" being declared a non-Indian by non-Indians. While the rationale of racial classification has always been wrong, it is a useful means of preventing intrusion into valuable territory, such as the art world.

Jack Forbes, professor of Native American studies at the University of California, Davis, presents another complexity in his story "Only Approved Indians Can Play: Made in USA." The story, which re-creates an unfortunately common occurrence in Indian country, reveals how those who should speak for and defend tribal ways share the same pangs of moral discontent as those they should oppose; they live in the same fog of indirection and uncertainty. The story is about a basketball game in which those who can exclude everyone else win without having to play the game at all. The tournament is restricted to players who are members of federally recognized tribes, and one team, which happens to have proper identification, challenges players on all the other teams who do not have proof of enrollment until all the other teams are barred from play. The basketball game is part of a complex and arbitrary society in which the players participate whether they serve or oppose it. The players administer the bureaucracy of existence to themselves as well as others in a world where they are never quite able to see clearly what it is they are accomplishing.

Forbes displays the players as examples of paradox and contradiction. But the principle of the story is irony. Nothing works as it should, and everything has a double meaning. The players not only are blind to their own fates and to the duality inherent in the human condition, but also function as "them." What Forbes attacks is the social order as a whole—Indians, whites, and the entire backdrop of culture around whose duplicities and paradoxes the game is organized.

The story satirizes issues that resulted from the politicization of Indian identity since the 1930s and the Indian Reorganization Act. Previously, the concept of blood quantum or degree of Indian ancestry was utilized more for purposes of achieving diversity by Indians than for purposes of diminishment. In fact, Indians routinely incorporated people from other groups or their descendants into their societies as a means of increase and diversification.

Indian portrayals of identity issues through the trope of mixed-blood are also drawn in James Welch's *The Death of Jim Loney,* Mourning Dove's *Cogewea,* Maria Campbell's *Halfbreed,* and Gerald Vizenor's *Griever,* but such portrayals are ultimately vastly underrepresented in the whole of contemporary literature. Unfortunately, as noted by William J. Scheick in *The Half-Blood,* the most famous portrayals of Indians in American literature are probably the villains, as typified by Blue Duck of Larry McMurtry's hugely popular recent novel and television miniseries, *Lonesome Dove.*

Blue Duck is characterized as extremely savage, but also somewhat mystical: "[He] had ranged the *llano* for so long, and butchered and raped and stolen so often, that superstitions had formed around him.

Some, particularly women, felt he couldn't die, and that their lives would never be safe."[25] When Texas Ranger W. F. Call finally catches up with the notorious villain, who is in jail waiting to be hanged, Blue Duck warns Call that he might just fly away. As Call approaches the jail on the day of the hanging, Blue Duck leaps out of an upper-floor window, looking at Call as he actually does fly through the air, albeit only to meet his death on the ground below.

While tenacious portraits such as these have undoubtedly done Indian people of all backgrounds much disservice, these characterizations are also subject to redescription. Writing can facilitate such redescription, as explained by Mary Clearman-Blew, author of *All but the Waltz* and *Balsamroot*: "There may be a parallel with the memoir writing — no longer is it enough to create the story, but also to create the teller of the story. . . . I think nothing is real until you write about it, including your sense of self. Experience is fiction, given embodiment by words. Illegitimacy, legitimacy — it isn't legitimate until you write it."[26] Balancing recalcitrant materials such as stereotypes, legal statutes, and racial and blood classifications by rewriting them is a tangible way for American Indians to begin imagining a better future. Intrinsic to this process is acceptance of the first principle of postapocalypse theory, the existence of the negative capability that is part of the larger picture of experience.

Review of such long-standing identity issues allows them to be placed in the context of the past, fulfilling one part of the ceremony of temporal unification of the past and future with the present. Naming and classifying the issues as part of an "authenticity debate" that has served certain purposes but now achieves diminishing returns is a concrete example of redescription that is responsive to the ever evolving nature of reality. A more detailed examination of what we mean when we talk about the authenticity debate will, I hope, begin to set the stage for imagining a better future for American Indians.

# American Indians, Authenticity, and the Future

MY AUNT, BY WHOM I WAS RAISED, WAS SKEPTICAL of certain individuals, including Crees, those included in the catchall category of "Breeds," those who drank, those who did not work, manipulative people, and most women, especially those who became involved with her boys. I was aware of her critical nature long before I understood anything about its origins, and it was only later that I understood, for example, that she didn't automatically hate our girlfriends.

I remember both my aunt and my grandmother telling stories of the mountain people traveling north who camped near the ranch in the fall. Although most were there to trade poles or horses for vegetables and beef, some were just "riding the grub line" and expected to receive food and water as a matter of hospitality. In fact, such hospitality was an unwritten law of the time and place, but given the extreme poverty that has always existed on the Fort Belknap Reservation, generosity had to be balanced with a firm hand.

The tension from resisting large numbers of people eating the family out of house and home was expressed through storytelling, resulting in some hilarious accounts of outwitting or outwaiting notorious freeloaders. Other stories were not funny, such as the time two ne'er-do-wells were turned away but returned after dark to lure my grandfather outside. They were on horseback and had taken their ropes down, which meant they intended to take their revenge by roping my grandfather and dragging him. He knew what they were up to, however, and told them to move on or he would shoot them.

My aunt's legendary mistreatment of potential daughters-in-law was harder to understand. Being related to certain families was enough to provoke instant disapproval of some young ladies, and those who made it through the front door were subjected to intense scrutiny. Any signs of laziness or other self-indulgence were unacceptable, and those who were interested in gaining favor needed to be ready to help but stay out of the way, be pleasant but know when to be quiet, and, most of all, exhibit no signs of being "man-crazy," the most egregious symptom of which was neglecting work by "chasing around."

My aunt and grandfather appeared unable to differentiate between outlaws and young girls. They were not naturally ornery, as some argued, but their circumstances were so harsh as to demand immediate action to head off potential trouble. In the case of unwanted guests, I imagine it was difficult to have things when so many others had nothing; in the case of romance, I now understand it is equally difficult to encourage young men in relationships for which they have little chance of providing food, shelter, and other necessities. Yet, these were the circumstances created by processes of genocide and acculturation under which my family lived.

Although these stories took place in the early to mid-1900s, the underlying self-critical mentality persists among Indian people. The primary reason seems to be that the most angry people are also the most frightened. There are often ample reasons for anger and fear, but those emotions are only helpful when directed at those who have the power to change social, economic, and environmental inequities.

In a recent seminar on Vine Deloria Jr., I encouraged graduate students to submit their final essays to a prominent American Indian scholarly journal. The reaction of such journals to submitted materials is varied, but they often provide copies of their readers' responses, which can prove valuable. In this particular case, however, a reviewer, whom I took to be an American Indian, mounted a personal attack, which the journal unwisely forwarded. The Indian-nationalist polemics continued for two-and-a-half single-spaced pages, ending with the statement: "So, all in all, it seems to me this essay is screwed up to the point of sheer irredeemability in just about every way possible. I could suggest that the author start over from scratch, but somehow I think it would be kinder and more productive — for Indians, if not for the author personally — to recommend that s/he find a completely different topic or set of topics to write about. Better yet, s/he might want to consider finding a whole new area of interest. Indians have enough problems without being subjected to any more of this kind of self-serving bullshit."[1] Obviously such remarks are more helpful to the reviewer and his/her own personal problems than to the author.

This example effectively demonstrates the dramatic cognitive dissonance involved — the academic community and its activities help, not attack, those seeking to understand worthwhile issues; indeed, for an academic journal to condone such behavior and language is troubling. What is more significant, however, is consideration of how the remarks might illustrate negative capability — if we can understand the mind of the reviewer and the motivation of the journal, we might be able to make something positive of a seemingly negative situation. In fact, this kind of abusive behavior has a long and complicated history that tends to hide issues vital to understanding Indian people.

For example, there are common refrains in discussions of inherited traditions as well as the contemporary lived experiences of tribal peoples. There are also other vitally important issues that remain strongly suppressed and are almost never discussed. The more common subjects have tended to orbit around a long-standing "authenticity" debate that is still firmly grounded in blood quantum, wherein an individual must usually prove one-quarter Indian blood and the higher the percentage of Indian blood the more authentic the individual is considered to be. Lately, however, the debate has also branched into discussions of whether the content of Indian writing is authentic, which opens up the new problem of who is qualified to judge. In addition, the debate ranges from expressions of personal frustration about who gets to be Indian to first-rate analyses of the problems related to authenticity.[2] Unfortunately, more tangible problems, such as genocide and what recent mainstream scholars have termed the *American Holocaust*, are still so strongly linked to fear and terror that American Indian scholars rarely mention them. We expect a transition from analysis to resolution of the issues, which has not yet taken place. Vine Deloria's analysis of the problem of Indian leadership in *Custer Died for Your Sins* (1969) remains a highly relevant study of matters related to authenticity, however, and serves as an excellent starting point for current discussion.

Deloria points out that discussions of authenticity are fueled by Indian cultural motifs: "In the old times as we have seen, a man's position rested primarily upon his ability to attract followers. Indians have come to rely on a strong leader and this in turn has created the War Chief complex," which is organized around personalities rather than issues.[3] Deloria feels it is the primary reason Indians have never been able to unite on a large scale, as exemplified in a typical discussion at national Indian · meetings: "The first Indian will announce that he lives in a one-room shack. He will be rebutted by an Indian educator who has lost his identity between two cultures. Another will agree about the two cultures and will immediately be refuted by an old timer fighting for his treaty rights who is simultaneously challenged because he doesn't speak for all the Indians" (213).

One consequence of these leadership patterns is that Indian leaders become quickly exhausted because their followers place absolute dependence upon them rather than share the burden. Another serious problem is that, "When national or regional unification is based upon the personality of the leader, insane jealousies develop which are fed by white elements hoping to weaken tribal alliances" (216).

We must remember that although traditional tribal-leadership patterns play an important role in Indians' tendency toward divisiveness, the mainstream has also contributed significantly through various "divide and conquer" strategies, such as the destruction of traditional means of existence and the subsequent creation of the Bureau of Indian Affairs, which provides less material goods and services than Indian people need to survive, forcing them to fight among themselves for those goods and services.

The authenticity debate has continued as a primary vehicle for many conversations by and about American Indians since Deloria published *Custer Died for Your Sins*. Two examples are Daniel F. Littlefield's article, "American Indians, American Scholars, and the American Literary Canon,"[4] and Arnold Krupat's "Scholarship and Native American Studies: A Response to Daniel Littlefield, Jr."

Both scholars identify issues and draw conclusions that provide much-needed perspective. Littlefield points out the ways academe has been self-serving in its treatment of the issues, substantiating Vine Deloria's observation that mainstream academics have latched onto Indians as a means of advancing their careers. Krupat sharpens the issues by categorizing underlying rhetorical strategies such as the double bind, essentialization, and cultural ownership. Although both articles are helpful, it would not be appropriate to suggest that either Littlefield's or Krupat's analysis of the authenticity debate resolves the issues.

One obvious reason is they both continue to operate within the closed circuit of the debate without providing a means of moving forward. It is one thing to thoroughly analyze a conversation, but it is another to put it into a historical context, identify the current manifestations of the issues, and synthesize effective action for the future. In fact, the authenticity debate defined in this manner provides an excellent example of unification of the past and future with the present. If contemporary discussions of authenticity, which tend to focus exclusively on the present, can evolve to include considerations of the past and the future, the necessary balance can be achieved.

At the present time the authenticity debate seems to have regressed to the time prior to the Littlefield-Krupat conversation, wherein the discussions often deteriorated into ad hominem attacks lacking helpful conclusions. As a result, as evidenced in a recent conversation devoted to American Indian writing, opportunities to constructively criticize American Indian intellectual activities consistently stall at the level of questioning authenticity, such as that of well-recognized "mixed-blood" writers.[5] Virtually all the established writers of the Native American Renaissance are "mixed-blood," and questioning their qualifications is useless.

Krupat, however, has effectively persisted with publication of *The Turn to the Native: Studies in Criticism and Culture*. Krupat's work has been useful not only in identifying and naming rhetorical strategies used in discussion of American Indian issues, but also in searching out theoretical frameworks by which American Indian literary critics can conduct comparative discussions with those involved in other literatures. For example, in *The Turn to the Native* he suggests comparing Kwame Anthony Appiah's notion of first- and second-stage postcolonial African novels to American Indian fiction. Krupat says N. Scott Momaday's *House Made of Dawn* and *The Ancient Child*, as well as Leslie Marmon Silko's *Ceremony* are examples of first-stage novels, describing them as "an ideological image of Indianness for Native Americans and for the rest of the world."[6] Krupat's suggestion regarding ideology is particularly weighty in this post–Cold War period, implying that American Indian worldviews, articulated effectively, have considerable potential to influence a new ideology.

A second-stage-type novel, described by Appiah as less celebratory, more critical, and with an element of delegitimation, accounts for later texts of the Native American Renaissance, including James Welch's *Winter in the Blood* and *The Death of Jim Loney*.[7] This distinction helps illuminate historic and underappreciated distinctions between writers of the northern plains, the southern plains, and those of the southwest Pueblo cultures.

The potential of such a discussion should be obvious. For example, as would seem appropriate, the distinction between northern plains, southern plains, and southwest writers is strongly tied to place. When Interior Secy. John Collier traveled west in the 1930s to investigate concerns about treatment of Indians, he fortuitously visited the Pueblos of the southwest. Impressed by the dignity and beauty of their cultures, he returned to Washington enthusiastic about lending support, and was instrumental in creating the Indian Reorganization Act. The Pueblo cultures remained largely intact because they were situated within great deserts perceived as being of no value to primarily agrarian settlers. Had Collier traveled to the verdant Great Plains, which bore the brunt of westward expansion, his reaction to the fragmented cultures might have produced a different result.

Because the plains cultures bear the mark of colonization so much more strongly, the works of Welch and Erdrich reflect a more realist worldview based in contemporary tribal configurations that does not authorize the return to tradition in the ways southwestern writers do. The obvious reason is that the traditional world of the plains tribes is simply not available to the same degree as the traditional world of the Pueblos, which is thriving. These kinds of differences are probably much more worthy of discussion within the authenticity debate than those that frequently focus on personalities.

These tribal differences are reflected in the ways Krupat brings Gerald Vizenor into the authenticity debate by commenting on Vizenor's contemporary tribal, postmodern views. Vizenor's sensibility is disturbing to many because it often departs from linear structures and creates characters that regularly transgress the bounds of standard behavior. On the central issue of authenticity, however, he engages more clearly, announcing in *The Heirs of Columbus* that it was mixed-blood, cross-blood mongrels who "created the best humans, we had that cross-blood wild bounce in our blood."[8]

Krupat clarifies his earlier writing on the subject of the implications of differentiation between the oral and the written for the study of Native oral literature by linking Vizenor to both oral tradition and the recent turn to autobiographical work: "Indeed, *Dead Voices* concludes with the strongest defense Vizenor has yet provided of the necessity of writing the oral tradition in the urban post-Indian era in the interest of healing and survivance." Central to the discussion of autobiography is Vizenor's concern with pronoun usage, in particular the use of the first-person singular: "the shift from 'I' to 'we' in *Dead Voices* bears as much on Gerald Vizenor's sense of identity as it does on that of a fictional character nicknamed Laundry Boy."[9] This line of inquiry provides another important example of the kinds of discussions that illuminate the subtleties in suppressed discourses rather than making hasty generalizations.

Vizenor's work suggests it is time to investigate the implications of the future to balance considerations of the past, and he perceives a postmodern form of oral tradition as a necessary element. This emphasis on older forms also suggests that "survivance" means survival in the most basic sense. If we can accept that the increasingly common ethnic warfare is a glimpse of our own future, we can begin to understand how

45

technology and theory may soon take a backseat to "survivance" and its conflation of survival and existence in a tribal-style "we."

Vizenor addresses later concepts of self, Indian and mainstream, suspicious of the limiting and coercive aspects of society, that have in critical ways turned to authenticity as a desideratum in place of sincerity. The ground for this view is not society or tribe, but exclusively the self, which seeks to achieve freedom in alienation from society. Language, for those who prize authenticity, has lost its value as a source of ethical truth or consolation and is valued instead as an agent of spiritual self-realization necessitating abandonment of social norms.

At the same time, to be acculturated in tribal communities is to acquire an aversion to self-reference, which opposes the postmodern move toward disregard of conditioning realities and the tearing of the social fabric. These conflicts exist at the deeper levels of the authenticity debate and have an exacerbating effect because they are so little understood. The erosion of social ties, both in mainstream U.S. culture and in Indian communities, and the elevation of individual autonomy and resentment of culture as essential conditions for achieving authenticity have promoted a false sense of being, which is the primary problem faced by both societies today.

These kinds of considerations regarding what is happening to the self in modern literature tie in with Vizenor's criticism of American Indian Movement (AIM) radicals who claim the atrocities endured by all tribal cultures by simply adopting the first-person plural. Krupat concludes that the decision was emblematic of Vizenor's desire "to commit himself to fighting for the survivance of tribal people with the pen rather than . . . the sword or gun."[10] Arguably, Vizenor's use of *we*, although inspired by his experience as a member of a small community, is concerned with social, racial, and economic inequities affecting Indians in general. Vizenor often uses *we* to refer to the secular community of the contemporary intelligentsia, which, for most urban and reservation Indian people, is alien and unresponsive.

It is certainly understandable that Krupat feels the need to tread lightly, given that he, like so many others, is attempting to occupy American Indian territory, but there are those who consider Vizenor's rhetorical strategies as a kind of elitist double-talk that prevents him from ever helping to resolve social, racial, and economic inequities. At the same time, he is openly critical of certain individuals, such as AIM members, many of whom have fought and literally died "in the trenches." Taking care to honor these modern warriors, while conducting persuasive and penetrating critical discourse, might soften what has been perceived as elitism.

In order to move toward more complete criticism we might consider the impulse to go beyond culture, in the sense of rejecting society in pursuit of the autonomous self. This situation has been analyzed by Lionel Trilling, who suggests that modern literature plays an adversarial, subversive role. Trilling describes a vital component of this subversion as an "angelism" that insists on direct access to the spirit by circumventing the conditions and circumstances of life, with the certain result of devaluing man's life in society. An attendant problem is erosion of the willpower to struggle with the important grounding of societal limitations to a fantasy of unfettered will characteristic of modern culture.[11]

Trilling, an intellectual marginalized much like American Indian intellectuals, developed an early Arnoldian conviction that literature promoted and clarified the moral life and taught people to fulfill themselves within the community. Toward the end of his career, however, and particularly in the youth culture of the sixties, he constantly found evidence to the contrary. As he probed the relationship of culture and literature, he saw that the aspects of modern literature that controverted his humanistic convictions were a natural outgrowth of a shift in the values animating the moral life, which he delineated as a movement from sincerity to authenticity. Trilling suggests his sense of authenticity in his assertion that the counterculture of the sixties "values highest those things experienced without intervention of rational thought and views irrationalism as a hallmark of authenticity."[12]

The central ideas of many conversations on Indian writing often turn on a similar form of authenticity, which then leads to failure to provide an adequate critical analysis of the dilemmas of contemporary Indian life. This can happen in a number of ways, an example of which can be found in many areas of ethnic study. As part of their early need to respond to the demand for ethnic studies, universities often placed ethnic scholars in positions of great responsibility without adequate attention to continuing development or other institutional support. Faced with the stress of extremely complicated situations, these scholars either have become academic transients or have resorted to combativeness to survive. In fact, virtually every American Indian academic I know either has regularly moved from job to job or has distanced him/herself from academe as soon as possible.

On the other hand, such behavior also exhibits a Keatsian negative capability. When dealing with bureaucracy, a certain level of hysteria must often be reached before anything can be accomplished. Similarly, the clash and conversation organized around issues of authenticity almost always provide the kinds of fireworks that at least make it difficult to ignore those issues.

If the authenticity debate can be explained as a kind of allegorical representative of the postmodern American Indian condition, it may finally find its appropriate context. Crucial to this is admitting fear and feelings of alienation associated with past events. In addition, it is important to turn such feelings into useful criticism directed outward to issues that need resolution, instead of simply intensifying self-criticism that can become self-hatred.

In order to move toward more positive and specific answers, it is necessary that existing work be completed by a larger constructive philosophical effort. We might begin with temporal unification of the past, present, and future by working to resolve the American intellectual middle class's "dramatic contradiction of its living with the greatest possibility (call it illusion) of conscious choice, its believing itself the inheritor of the great humanist and rationalist tradition, and the badness and stupidity of its actions."[13]

First, the genocide perpetrated by colonizing Europeans upon the indigenous peoples of the Americas must be acknowledged and reasonable compensation made for the tremendous losses. Arguments that suggest Indians simply forget about their loss and forgo acknowledgment of atrocities or proper compensation are unacceptable and will only prolong the resolution of critical issues for both Indians and the mainstream. Then, it is crucial to consider carefully what is happening to the self in modern mainstream and ethnic cultures and how that contributes to gross social, racial, and economic inequities.

The role of modern literature in the process of change is of primary importance. Literature by and about American Indians is a counterbalance to the destructive aspects of colonization, revealing a pragmatic and humanist authorial personality determined to constitute and preserve American Indians by writing. One example is Jonathan Boyarin's analysis of the relations of Jews and Indians in *Storm from Paradise: The Politics of Jewish Memory*. Boyarin discusses how the European and American mainstreams constantly eulogize the other's victims and the concomitant juxtaposition of "native" voices inside the respective empires as a way of resisting. Boyarin states unequivocally that contrasting fictions by French Jew Patrick Modiano and American Indian Gerald Vizenor are "the voices of survivors, written after genocide, on the soil of genocide."[14]

The problem of the genocide perpetrated against the indigenous peoples of the Americas, to say nothing of the scope of that genocide, as more fully documented by David Stannard in *American Holocaust*, has yet to be addressed on any but the most basic level. Nor has there been sufficient discussion of the continued genocide under which most of the survivors of the American Holocaust still exist. Furthermore, until American Indians can speak of such things as directly as do Boyarin and Stannard, they will not have fully recovered their sacred duty to community, and their discourse will remain incomplete.

In Stannard's words, "The destruction of the Indians of the Americas was, far and away, the most massive act of genocide in the history of the world."[15] One might think that such a strong declaration would provoke corrective action, yet that has not proved true. An intrinsic problem with such a statement is that it institutionalizes experience, leading to a betrayal of the original experience and of the present articulation, by creating a false sense of self gained by vicarious (easy) experience.

Stannard attempts to resist this phenomenon by layering details, such as telling of "dogging," or using packs of trained dogs to kill Indians, a favorite sport of the conquistadores. One story tells of "Leoncico, or 'little lion,' a . . . cross between a greyhound and a mastiff. . . . Leoncico tore the head off an Indian leader in Panama. . . . Heads of human adults do not come off easily, so the authors of *Dogs of the Conquest* seem correct in calling this a 'remarkable feat' . . ." (83).

The overwhelming magnitude of such horrors visited on the indigenous peoples of the Americas tends to obliterate both the writer's and the reader's sense of its truly terrible human element. Older estimates place the Indian population in the United States at approximately 800,000 at the time of discovery, with approximately 295,000 remaining at the turn of the nineteenth century. More recent estimates, however, place the size of the precontact (between Indians and Europeans) population of the Americas at around 145 million for the hemisphere as a whole and about 18 million for the area north of Mexico.[16] By 1890, 95 percent of this original population had been killed (x). As I have become aware that hundreds more tribes existed than I originally thought, and of the U.S. government's overwhelming need to downplay its violent role in the conquest of this country, I find the larger figures more believable. The continuing process of genocide is evidenced by statistics such as the rate for alcohol-caused mortality on modern Indian reservations, which is more than 900 percent higher than the national average (257).

Obliteration of the human element by such magnitude can be resisted by recognizing, in Stannard's terms, that "We must do what we can to recapture and to try to understand, in human terms, what it *was* that was crushed, what it *was* that was butchered."[17] The Sand Creek massacre, perpetrated by Colorado militia commander Col. John Chivington against a small band of Cheyenne and Arapaho consisting mainly of women and children, on November 29, 1864, stands out. From the testimony of a cavalryman following the slaughter comes this harrowing biographical representation:

There was one little child, probably three years old, just big enough to walk through the sand. The Indians had gone ahead, and this little child was behind following after them. The little fellow was perfectly naked, travelling on the sand. I saw one man get off his horse, at a distance of about seventy-five yards, and draw up his rifle and fire—he missed the child. Another man came up and said, "Let me try the son of a bitch; I can hit him." He got down off his horse, kneeled down and fired at the little child, but he missed him. A third man came up and made a similar remark, and fired, and the little fellow dropped.[18]

## American Indians, Authenticity, and the Future

Genocide means the intentional killing of women and children — for no population can survive if its women and children are destroyed. The United States has never properly acknowledged its participation in such indiscriminate killing, nor the theft of nearly 3 billion acres of Indian lands, offering instead palliatives such as "citizenship," the Indian Reorganization Act, and the careful doling out of small amounts of money by the Indian Claims Commission. The inequity of such reparations remains to be adjudicated, along with other questions of moral bookkeeping, such as why European Jewish victims have been acknowledged with the U.S. Holocaust Memorial when no such acknowledgment exists for American Indians. Until such matters are addressed, the discourse of American Indians, in particular, will not have achieved morality of the kind that could result from directing all the available force of kindred minds at the crude mass of experience in an endeavor to extract meaning from it. Although sympathetic "others" have assisted in opening up this discussion, it is vital that American Indians themselves carry such personal issues forward for resolution as a means of establishing self-efficacy.

Moving beyond the many divisive effects of colonialism is essential to the well-being of American Indians, especially those still living in the midst of ongoing genocide in rural and urban ghettos. N. Scott Momaday has said unequivocally that we are what we imagine ourselves to be, and someone must imagine a better future for American Indians and then ask for it. Placing this discussion in a postmodern context is a way to acknowledge the fear and terror generated by the process of colonization upon the indigenous peoples of the Americas, while ultimately pointing to ways of imagining a better future.

Certain postmodern texts herald a better future in that they prompt readers to confront their fears of loss or diminishment by allowing other entities to be acknowledged as "persons." For example, regaining a conception of nature that permits us to genuinely consider the consequences of our interactions with the environment would permit refiguring the kinds of persons we might become. The postmodern work of Gerald Vizenor, Ursula LeGuin, Octavia Butler, and William Gibson presses the boundaries of personhood not only by decentering the idea of identity or individuality, but also by suggesting that personhood is not exclusively human. Most important, this inclusive concept of personhood is not postmodern at all, but actually a premodern cornerstone of American Indian traditional worldviews.

Patricia Linton, in "The 'Person' in Postmodern Fiction: Gibson, LeGuin, and Vizenor," notes Arnold Krupat's suggestion that postmodernism has had a salutary effect on the reception of Native American literature because it has accustomed readers to more varied literary insights and strategies.[19] Linton identifies William Gibson's *Neuromancer* as an excellent postmodern novel emphasizing matriarchy and illegitimate children, two themes common to Native American literature. In *Neuromancer* the overarching consciousness of the book, Wintermute, seeks to unite with his alter ego, Neuromancer, an expression of feminine concern for relationship rather than the patriarchal concern for control. Linton cites Vizenor and LeGuin for their different definitions of "self," and reminds us of the all-too-human tendency to be too anthropocentric to recognize any natural agency except our own.

Postmodern Indian storytellers also deal with a world often presented as being too complicated to understand. Some, like Gerald Vizenor, have found ways to extrapolate from oral tradition to create work similar to other postmodern writers such as LeGuin, Butler, and Gibson. Other Indian writers, such as Momaday, Welch, Silko, and Erdrich, have helped combat the feeling of helplessness in the face of events by portraying worlds in which relationship to society, personal choice, and action count. For example, the most important "action" in all these texts consists of figuring out how to relate to family, as opposed to the valuation of self-gratification, wealth, and violence found in most mainstream stories. At the heart of this writing is a polemic about America built on a pattern of observed detail that also seeks to record the worldviews of a number of distinct tribal groups. These writers bring a sensibility to their work that is balanced by honoring a world of inherited traditions as well as engaging the world encountered in daily life. Their work is informed but not elitist; it is studious but not unintelligible to those it might help most; finally, it balances the red road of Indian metaphysics with the black road of worldly experience.

American Indian literature has been shaped by the literary deconstruction of the 1980s, as well as the subsequent self-reflexive turn to postcolonial studies of the 1990s. Postcolonial critics in countries such as Canada and Australia, where conflicting nationalist ideologies openly affect literary debate, address the lack of balance in various new theoretical enterprises. In many cases, there is a persistently unequal distribution of power apparent even in those discourses in which the subject is power.

Unequal distribution of power has resulted in debates such as those centered on the meaning of multiculturalism and related categories of pluralism, diversity, and heterogeneity. Although the term *multicultural* has a certain utility, it has also been the subject of ridicule for representing token participation in activities relating to ethnic groups while carefully maintaining the privileges of majority culture. Such a double stance leads to ambiguity, and often absurdity. David Goldberg provides additional explanation:

Between the homogenizing, assimilative thrust of conservative (or weak) multiculturalism and the condescending tolerant pluralism of liberalism's managed multiculturalism (which . . . lumps together homogeneous "people of color"), it should be evident that certain kinds of heterogeneity are experienced socially and academically as dangerous. And indeed they are. Heterogeneity may be dangerous . . . because it places distinct limits on the comfort and easiness of the established and already ordered, of the familiar and the controlled.[20]

There are many perplexing questions surrounding multiculturalism, such as how to broaden a term such as *American* through the writings of various ethnic groups; whether to include race, class, gender, and sexual orientation within the definition of multiculturalism; and how to understand insider/outsider politics that inform multiculturalism. Such questions are often found in literary representations, which, although not identical with lived experience, often explore the boundaries that separate different forms of discourse.

For example, *Other Solitudes: Canadian Multicultural Fictions,* edited by Linda Hutcheon and Marion Richmond, combines analysis of the literary works of an ethnically diverse group of writers with interviews conducted with the authors. The resulting dialogues are often critical of political structures and economic systems. The text portrays Canada as being invested in the preservation and enhancement of multiculturalism, although only in the sense of being the ground from which all other ethnic groups diverge. However, *Other Solitudes* also reveals certain failures to create a multicultural society in Canada. Most important, the writing/interview format deconstructs the single-author text by allowing the writers to speak for themselves.

Janice Williamson's 1993 *Sounding Differences: Conversations with Seventeen Canadian Women Writers* also employs an interview/conversation structure that allows the writers to refer to each other's lives and work, while maintaining dialogues with Williamson. This is a great way to emphasize the importance of individual voices speaking both for themselves and in dialogue, which can also be seen as fundamental support for the emergence of contemporary autobiography. This experiment with egalitarian interchanges recognizes pluralism as a method of subverting literary canons, in addition to its usual function of maintaining cultural superiority.

Williamson emphasizes spoken words as much as written work, resulting in a strong sense of shared discussion that allows the writers/ speakers to theorize their own identities. For example, Kristjana Gunnars, in "The Prowler," writes in short, numbered passages that oblige the reader (the prowler) to thread his or her way through disjointed clips in order to construct a narrative, thus enumerating the difficulties faced by immigrant Icelandic women. Jeannette Armstrong focuses on problems of agency; for example, what does it mean for non-Native writers to write from the Indian point of view? Armstrong joins the critical question with gender issues by inquiring whether there are different creative processes for female and male Native writers, then argues that choosing a male narrator for her novel *Slash* is discretionary and need not be tied to knee-jerk loyalty to feminism. Both Gunnars and Armstrong help to illustrate the importance of process compared to product and to demonstrate diversity through both individual communication and theory.

*Sounding Differences* gives prominent positions to a number of individuals interested in experimenting with fiction in postmodern ways. In particular, each writes in a mode that has been called "fiction/the-

ory," designed to expose "the internal incoherence of absolute categories."[21] These kinds of postmodern disruptions of binary oppositions
and dismantling of various hierarchies serve as excellent examples for
the direction of the American Indian postcolonial project as well as models for a central aim of our particular multiculturalism.

Further direction is provided by Julia Emberley's *Thresholds of Difference: Feminist Critique, Native Women's Writings, Postcolonial Theory*.
Emberley attacks racism and ethnocentrism, focusing specifically on
Native populations and the problems that occur when those in power
speak for the disfranchised. Emberley defines postcolonialism as an ideological way of configuring the First World's "symbolic debt to the so-
called Third World," and suggests that feminism should address part of
this debt through Marxist theory.[22]

Emberley stresses concrete experience as crucial to all feminist
methodologies, which echoes American pragmatism. One result is that
her analyses of Jeannette Armstrong's *Slash*, Beatrice Culleton's *In
Search of April Raintree*, and Maria Campbell's *Halfbreed* all combine
history and fiction. The bridging of disciplines illustrates how oral
tradition disrupts some of the formal devices of conventional Western
narratives and suggests how collisions in sign systems, generic categories, and economic structures can point toward a different cognitive
mapping (25).

Finally, and of great importance, is the fact that within the concept
of heterogeneity as reflected in *Other Solitudes, Sounding Differences*
and *Thresholds of Difference* there is a politeness that reflects a more tolerant view of identity, a caution against advocating politics of difference
within notions of community, and an emphasis on the contradictions in
feminist practice that are subsumed under abstract categories such as
difference. As a result, texts such as *Slash, In Search of April Raintree*,
and *Halfbreed* broaden what has been conventionally included in the
category of Indian literature. Similarly, by breaking down the distribu-
tions of power, the authors are able to position heterogeneity so that it
challenges "the mythical inward obsessiveness of purity with the generative energy of impurity, the projection of natural normativity with
abnormal transgression, the limit of the Same with the transformative
renewability of the possible and the novel."[23]

The texts are valuable to discussions of American Indian literary trajectory for the ways they suggest American Indian literature and criticism can move forward: supplementing univocal scholarly analysis with dialogues as much as possible to avoid single-author texts; blending theory and fiction as a means of exposing the internal incoherence of absolute categories; paying attention to class struggles in the way articulated by Bronwen Wallace, who said: "The academic feminists who make me nervous are those who are not engaged in the world, who just sit and write some interesting papers about feminist thought but who have never talked to a waitress in their lives";[24] working back and forth between history and fiction in ways that contest generic boundaries and illustrate how oral tradition disrupts some of the formal devices of conventional Western narratives; and taking care to practice a politeness that will establish a much more tolerant view of identity.

Indeed, the foundation of American Indian sensibility is based on inherently polite unified forms wherein the images and the realities of the circle are dominant. For example, to paraphrase my old friend Charles Woodard, as part of the circle, one is supported on both sides and connected all the way around, in level contact with everyone else. No backs are turned. No one is "ahead" or "behind." One need not be apprehensive about one's "place" relative to other places — all places are equal. And the smallest circle is part of a larger circle, and on and on, to create the whole circle of life that is creation.

These kinds of pragmatic American Indian notions of balancing inherited traditions with experience have potential to result in worldviews intimately tied to everyday life. These worldviews can reflect valuable lessons, such as the facts that each of us is obligated to help effect the good of the human community and that human problems must be understood and solved in their environmental contexts.

Imagination, not argument, is most effective in achieving widespread changes in attitude and opinion. This observation is substantiated by recent revivals of interest in narrative in such diverse fields as history and medical science. American Indians have always based their existences in narrative, and it is in their use of such stories that all people can find lessons for their own existence. In the words of Thought-Woman, the spider: "I will tell you something about stories. . . . They aren't just entertainment. . . . You don't have anything if you don't have the stories. . . ."[25]

In certain regards, the Indian story has started to lean dangerously toward the kinds of separation and division that have begun to tear European and Asian cultures apart. Especially within scholarship, there is a tendency for American Indians to attack one another, and to create strong internal boundaries instead of highlighting relationships. On the other hand, there are countervailing forces existing, for example, within American Indian fiction that tend to reflect equally powerful notions of positive self-identity, family, community, and relationship to environment.

Both discourses, however, tend to avoid certain issues that can benefit from being placed in the context of history, present circumstances, and anticipation of the future. If such unification can be undertaken seriously, new ways of gathering up the best parts of American Indian existence can begin to be imagined. Although the process might seem daunting, excellent beginnings can be found in the existing work of American Indian scholars and creative writers.

# Vine Deloria Jr.
# *Reconstructing the*
# *Logic of Belief*

**MY FIRST INKLING THAT WE ARE TRULY A** killing species came with Francis Ford Coppola's *Godfather* movies, wherein the concept of family was associated with murder as a business strategy. Notions of family became further vexed for me by the awareness that the highest percentage of homicides are committed by family members. If members of families kill one another routinely, it is no wonder that other groups of humans, who do not know or care for one another, can kill each other wholesale.

Having accepted these realities, I read Philip Gourevitch's recent accounts of genocide between Hutus and Tutsis in Rwanda, in the *New Yorker*, a magazine that occasionally ventures outside the world of arts and letters to examine the world upon which art is based. I am morbidly fascinated by such accounts because they seem to be the norm rather than the exception to historical human behavior, and because I am of American Indian background. I have had to delve into obscure scholarship to find discussions regarding genocide committed against American Indians, but I still feel the silent terror associated with extermination, the backdrop of my upbringing on the Fort Belknap Reservation of Montana.

## Vine Deloria Jr.: Reconstructing the Logic of Belief

Although global communications make it increasingly clear that genocide, which I once understood was to be viewed as committed only by German Nazis, is common, there is little information regarding why or what might be done about it. After a long period of study it has been personally significant to discover the best information regarding various aspects of genocide comes from Vine Deloria Jr., a Sioux Indian intellectual who is a member of the department of history at the University of Colorado, Boulder. Although I am sure the term *Indian intellectual* remains an oxymoron in the mainstream perception, it seems fitting that a surviving member of a nearly obliterated culture is an expert on matters associated with obliteration.

The key to understanding the postapocalypse situation of American Indians is the work of Vine Deloria Jr. Possessed of a grasp of tribal history, Deloria also understands the meaning of what has gone before in light of present events. Critical in ways that urge both Indians and the mainstream to come to grips with their shared destiny, Deloria continually resists thinking in terms that fail to respect the complexity of natural laws. Although some attempt to emulate Deloria, few are able to achieve his pragmatic results.

In his book *Tribal Secrets: Vine Deloria, Jr., John Joseph Mathews, and the Recovery of American Indian Intellectual Traditions*, Robert Warrior, another Indian intellectual and a professor at Stanford University, describes Vine Deloria as being involved in "a search, at once pragmatic and idealistic, for answers to the problems of Native communities and the world as a whole."[1] In fact, this duality is but one of several with which Deloria engages, as he works back and forth between American Indian and mainstream worldviews.

The results of Deloria's multifaceted style are difficult for audiences accustomed to European-style linear thinking and writing, which is familiar but wherein reality is modified freely to reflect not natural order but anthropocentric ideal principles of a perfect mind or soul. Deloria instead presents reality as it is actually encountered, in unorganized bits and pieces flowing over and around perception like fast-moving water. This process is nonlinear, and reflective in some ways of what has come to be known as American Indian–style circular, accretive thinking, which is more like an accumulative spiral. In addition,

Deloria insists that where we live is much more important than we realize.

Deloria has undertaken a confrontational moral criticism that seeks to evaluate aspects of American Indian and mainstream cultures in terms of their usefulness in relation to human life. As a result, Indians and non-Indians alike get a strong dose of Uncle Vine wielding a Heideggerian understanding that being — coming to be, arising, being born — is primary; on the other hand, presence — that which is present, that which already exists — is derivative. He deconstructs anthropocentrism, asserting instead that human beings are indeed but children of the natural world, and that our everyday mode of being is an outward dispersal of ourselves toward the earth from whence we have come. This anxious being-toward-death is one of the absolute conditions of our existence, and it has great significance because it causes us to react in extreme ways to the sense of loss associated with death.

For example, Robert Warrior points out Deloria's argument that "early Christians redefined community as not existing in a particular place, but in a time not yet present" (132). As a result, many individuals considered their time on earth a waiting period prior to their real lives in "heaven." This, combined with Christian theology that advertises a bad end for this world anyway, encourages these same individuals to devalue and exploit it. Similarly, because we are sentient enough to fear our own deaths, we devalue and exploit one another in complicated rituals of sacrifice that we attempt to rationalize as moral wars or justifiable genocides.

Deloria's criticism of human nature and its religious institutions might be further understood in light of the postmodern philosopher Bernd Magnus's use of philosophy, the self-proclaimed representative of representation, as the frame for Nietzsche's claim that truth is the sort of error, the sort of falsification of fluid becoming, of which human beings are inordinately fond. Beginning by translating Nietzsche's assertion that God is dead as meaning philosophy must give up its position as *the* arbiter of representational claims, Magnus sharpens his point with an epigram from Wittgenstein, *Philosophical Investigations* #621: "When I raise my arm, my arm goes up. . . . What is left over if I subtract the fact that my arm goes up from the fact that I raise my arm?"

## Vine Deloria Jr.: Reconstructing the Logic of Belief

Magnus explains the central point of Wittgenstein's question as marking the difference between an intentional action and a mere bodily movement such as a twitch or reaction, with both question and explanation becoming a means of raising the question, "If from our current vocabulary we could subtract our current vocabulary, what, if anything, remains left over?" Magnus then suggests three responses:

1. *Whether it is the right vocabulary* (i.e., whether our current self and world descriptions — taken as a whole — are correct, are true in an unqualified, correspondence sense; whether what we claim to know *is* knowledge; whether our morality is the right one; and whether our sense of the ideal life is the correct perception and description of it);
2. *Nothing remains left over — acknowledged with nostalgia, regret, or a sense of loss;*
3. *Nothing remains left over — acknowledged without nostalgia, regret, or a sense of loss.*[2]

Magnus suggests that the third response is compatible with Nietzsche's suggestion that philosophy stop assuming to understand and speak for natural laws by utilizing some sort of final vocabulary of its own making.

Such final vocabularies, insisting on a kind of authenticity that leaves no room for difference or diversity, can be severely limiting, which Deloria actively resists. Relinquishing final vocabularies, however, is complicated by the regret, or sense of loss, that inevitably seems to follow. An example of the consequences of mismanaged sense of loss is found in Magnus's contemporary Giles Gunn's discussion of cultural conflict. Gunn describes the potential for basic human incompatibility that tends to increase dramatically when placed in cultural contexts such as Serbs and Muslims, or Israelis and Syrians, or Zulus and Xhosas, or Armenians and Azerbaijanis, or Iraquis and Iranians, or Poles and Gypsies, and in his observation that, in the face of such seemingly intractable culture conflicts, most liberal therapies seem ineffective. There is, in Gunn's view, however, a place to start:

[By] controlling the effects of that pervasive psychocultural process known as scapegoating where, as Kenneth Burke long ago reminded us, we transform others into sacrificial objects for the ritual unburdening of our own unwanted vices. A horrific practice that is almost endemic in human history because of the effective relief it provides for the sense of ambivalence, inadequacy, and stain that attends virtually any human life, scapegoating turns cultural essentialism into a mechanism of cultural victimage by not only saddling "the other" with the unassimilated residue of one's own childhood phobias and insecurities but also rendering the cultural "other" virtually opaque to anything it might mediate from beyond itself.[3]

Gunn proposes pragmatism as part of a therapy for dealing with scapegoating, suggesting such victimization be approached as a disease whose origins lie in the threat of loss.

Pragmatism, like psychoanalysis, can be used to treat the threat of loss by encouraging the ability to mourn. Mourning is the process by which the self can achieve psychological maturity by "sacrificing the security of defining the self in terms of some common set of fixed symbols that once organized, or at least once were presumed to organize, much of communal life, for the sake of trying to refashion oneself out of such new forms of subjectivity and sociality as emerge from a relaxation of its constraints."[4] Mourning opens up a new emotional, intellectual, and cultural space for the creation and enjoyment of new meanings. This is essentially work of the imagination, where loss can be redescribed as self-enhancement and where we can utilize our capacity to project ourselves into forms of life different from our own and to see ourselves from the perspective of others.

An example of redescribing loss is found in Deloria's perception of death and religion: "The singular aspect of Indian tribal religions was that almost universally they produced people unafraid of death. It was not simply the status of warrior in the tribal life that created a fearlessness of death. Rather the integrity of communal life did not create an artificial sense of personal identity that had to be protected and preserved at all costs."[5] This feature of American Indian pragmatism echoes Indian articulation of the necessity to balance considerations of the past with those of contemporary lived experience that comes from their post-apocalypse situation.[6]

The opening up of new space for the creation and enjoyment of new meanings is significant to Deloria's work. For example, in *God Is Red*, Deloria relates a story told by Dr. Charles Eastman, the famous Sioux physician:

A missionary once undertook to instruct a group of Indians in the truths of his holy religion. He told them of the creation of the earth in six days, and of the fall of our first parents by eating an apple.

The courteous savages listened attentively, and, after thanking him, one related in his turn a very ancient tradition concerning the origin of maize. But the missionary plainly showed his disgust and disbelief, indignantly saying: "What I delivered to you were sacred truths, but this that you tell me is mere fable and falsehood!"

"My Brother," gravely replied the offended Indian, "it seems that you have not been well grounded in the rules of civility. You saw that we, who practice these rules, believed your stories; why, then, do you refuse to credit ours?"[7]

Refusing to credit the stories of American Indians amounts to refusing to open up new space. By opening the space wherein the stories of American Indians and the mainstream reside to critical examination, Deloria drives toward a rationality that obtains when persuasion is substituted for force. He is saying that if care is taken to provide for free and open dialogic exchange, truth and rationality will result.

There are similarities between Deloria's Indian worldview and mainstream Euramerican thinking that has come to be known as pragmatism, a unique blending that is emblematic of a process world cultures will have to master if they are to survive. Such pragmatism insists on a precise description of the interaction between the mind and experience, asserts that the world of ideas be intimately tied to everyday life, and advances the idea that those who have the opportunity to engage in intellectual pursuits have an obligation to society to use their training and ability to help other people. This is different from the Western tradition, within which, from Plato to Hegel, intellectual operations of the mind were thought to reflect some sort of ideal principles of a perfect mind or soul. Perhaps most important, pragmatism seeks to address tangible situations in the present environment and dismisses any attempt to establish a correspondence with absolute values that allow continued destruction of that environment.[8]

Because Deloria takes the world as he finds it, there is a quality to his writing that is unfamiliar to readers of European-style texts. The natural world is not organized by theme or genre, but rather tends to happen all at once, revealing meaning only in accretive patterns and rhythms. Furthermore, experience is rude, never pretending to be other than it is, and never attempting to become something else through language. Deloria signifies upon all this and more, beginning with the title of his first book, *Custer Died for Your Sins*.

The title invites mainstream culture to consider the possibility it has transgressed sacred bounds while substituting a figure we now recognize as a fool, George Armstrong Custer, for the putative savior Jesus Christ. Less explicit, but probably even more confrontational, is an embedded suggestion of the need for salvation of an entire nation, a nation dependent on a religious framework powerless to guide it toward any workable solutions. Among other reactions, I have observed graduate students weep openly in response to the power of such elements of play, ridicule, judgment, and assertions of truth as they begin to read Deloria.

These same readers are often the ones who become most devoted to Deloria as they come to understand how American Indian trickster tales often attacked their own chiefs who were unjust, deceitful, or greedy, and how his style brings otherwise flat social criticism to life. In addition, as students become more sensitive to the ways European-style rhetorical strategies distort reality to achieve textual smoothness, or closure, they develop appreciation of Deloria's problem-solving schema that ranks issues according to their urgency in terms of the individuals and communities they affect, and that refuses to provide the too simple answers of yet another final vocabulary.

Within this schema Deloria undertakes temporal unification of the past and future with the present by explicating the history underlying current affairs, while suggesting more effective strategies for the future regarding social and economic realities, legal issues, and matters of spirituality among American Indians and mainstream peoples. An example of a helpful suggestion is Deloria's description of Amish and Mormon communities: "the Amish and perhaps the Mormons show how successfully communities can be established and maintained when they are restricted to ethnic communities residing in specific locations and preserving specific religious doctrines and ceremonial forms. The rest of Christendom and Indian religious and political leadership would do well to look at these groups as having made a realistic decision to perpetuate themselves as a community."[9]

Mocking excess is a sacred duty to the American Indian trickster-critic, and Deloria frames criticism of mainstream snobbery and moral self-righteousness with discussion of anthropologists: "into each life, it is said, some rain must fall. . . . Indians have anthropologists. . . ."[10] This kind of reflection becomes a larger criticism of Western thought and culture, a major reversal of scholarship and subject accomplished as an American Indian ethnography of Euramerican intellectual and religious lifeways, in his 1973 book, *God Is Red*.

*God Is Red* provides a systematic Indian response to the fundamentals of Western, Euramerican historiography, philosophy, theology, social criticism, and political theory. At various junctures Deloria offers new ways of understanding the world while suggesting the inadequacy of various Western modes of discourse. In one instance, he demonstrates that a historical interpretation assuming an alien invasion of a superior culture explains much of biblical history as well as accepted scientific explanations do. The point is not to assert belief in the existence of extraterrestrial beings, but to suggest that these same historical methods have often been used by non-Indian scholars to interpret and explain American Indian realities. In other instances, Deloria offers hermeneutical reflections intended as no more preposterous than the generally accepted solutions offered in Western scientific and social-scientific explanations of the world. Insofar as these so-called scientific explanations of the world have been used to signify American Indian existence in terms controlled by the mainstream, Deloria's supposititious arguments are useful challenges.

The most powerful aspect of *God Is Red* is its articulation of enduring natural categories of Indian cultures, especially systematic analysis of the distinction between spatiality and temporality as culturally discrete ways of being in the world, the communitarian-individualist difference between Indian and Euramerican cultures, and the realization that absolute principles should usually give way to a paradigm of reality that prioritizes context over content.

Deloria points out that history is often the justification for ideas that can overcome good sense and that in a world in which time is collapsed by such things as high-tech communications, "it must be spaces and places that distinguish us from one another, not time nor history." Good sense can take the form of considering the efficacy of balancing what people believe to be true with what they actually experience as true: "Spatial thinking requires that ethical systems be related directly to the physical world and real human situations, not abstract principles." [11]

In this sense, tribal religions may be useful in approaching certain world problems because they are linked to the landscape, which provides "identification of the specific location and lands where the religious event that created community took place. And . . . [tribal religions] stand by the historical nature of the event; it [religion] should never back off and disclaim everything while becoming furious with other peoples for not believing its claim" (122). Here Deloria refers to the tendency of Christians to insist that a chronology of nonexistent events constitutes an important historical time line that is superior to any other explanation of human experiences. Similar distortions of reality allow the long-term destruction of the environment in the name of short-term profit, or allow genocide to be the product of religious difference; being "grounded" by relationships to places where significant events actually occurred provides a way to avoid such results.

The second enduring category of American Indian cultures is community. Deloria states, "It is in the conception of community that Indian tribal religions have an edge on Christianity" (210). American Indians have a healthier perception of death based on belief in the community's continuity — in both earthly and spiritual worlds — and in stable identity that allows extending to other communities the dignity of distinct existence. This is in opposition to the mainstream conception of community as "rather transitory locations for the temporary existence of wage earners. . . . People come and go as the economics of the situation demand" (214). Again, Deloria suggests Amish people as examples of how modern communities can be established and maintained, by being structured as ethnic communities residing in specific locations and preserving specific religious doctrines and ceremonial forms that are not subject to the changes and novelties of popular culture.

When cultural context, time, and place are prioritized over content, new emotional, intellectual, and cultural space is opened for the creation and enjoyment of new meanings.[12] For example, "in understanding the corporation as a form of tribalism, a number of new paths of understanding are made possible."[13] This is another of Deloria's suggestions, now more than thirty years old, that will soon be put to the test as the result of welfare reform. We can only hope the nation will not turn away from its needy, as Deloria observes it turned away from the concept of the brotherhood of man when the civil rights movement forced those issues.

Other paths include resisting the tendency to make principles absolute, as well as avoiding extreme polarities that do not and should not exist in conceiving of difference. Bounded spheres of difference are desirable, so long as the boundaries are permeable, like human skin, rather than impenetrable, like fortress walls. The human-skin metaphor better envisions inclusion rather than exclusion, and expansion rather than diminishment, as part of modeling efficiency in social and economic structures.

If the mainstream can consider certain aspects of tribal worldviews as additions to the workable aspects of its existing structures, and if it can do so without the sense of loss, nostalgia, and regret that often results in hugely destructive projections of fear and insecurity, significant progress will have been made toward instituting a new and practicable national religion. In his social criticism, Deloria models certain aspects of American Indian cultures as ways to achieve feasible ideals by which a community identifies itself within a certain place over a period of time.

Other pragmatic and useful suggestions can be found in Deloria's *Metaphysics of Modern Existence*, which seeks to join an alternative view of history and science, as seen through the eyes and memories of American Indians, with those of the mainstream. In *Red Earth, White Lies*, Deloria expands on the need for such an exchange of views between American Indians and Western science, suggesting "a reconstructed logic of belief which rejects the notion of single truths."[14] As the scientific community increasingly looks to tribal beliefs to supplement scientific perceptions of social and environmental problems, the practicality of criticizing established accounts of many things, and of urging Western science to pluralize, becomes more obvious.

Although Deloria is often described as being sarcastic and more critical than helpful, his work increasingly seems in tune with modern revisions of scientific absolutes generating from new knowledge provided by such technology as the Hubble telescope. For example, he has long advocated serious consideration of catastrophic events as explanations of major world events presented in obscure ways in world poetics. Observing comets impact another planet lends much credence to the possibility of similar events causing the disappearance of dinosaurs as well as the floods depicted in the Christian Bible and in Indian oral tradition.

In addition, Deloria's rhetorical strategies seem more effective than "smoother" mainstream-academic styles of writing, of which he is certainly capable. His style may be considered nonacademic, fragmented, and incomplete, or even caustic, but such rhetorical strategies are appropriate for audiences who have come to believe social criticism must be grounded in some sort of transcendental argument or exotic theory. If the thinking of all peoples can be liberated from the bondage of specific pictures of inquiry, and if we can put aside sets of metaphors and final vocabularies, all of which aspire to become *the* theory of representation, progress can be made. Deloria deflates all absolute representations, making possible his assertion that American Indians not only fit in the modern world, but also make a valuable contribution to it.

Illuminating genocide, such as that which is ongoing in Rwanda, is a courageous and remarkable act. We are now aware that such things happen, and that they have happened throughout recorded history. We have thus completed one part of the healing ceremony American Indians have practiced for thousands of years, which is the temporal unification of the past and the future with the present, that is, we are aware of what has already happened and now must look to the future. One way we can do this is by considering the causes of genocide and what might be done to interrupt the cycle, a form of considering the present as the past of a better-imagined future.

If we can set aside final vocabularies that assume to have all the answers, without the sense of loss that calls for the sacrifice of others; if we can realize that the sliding scale of contextualizing situations as we encounter them and applying the useful information available from all cultures is superior to beating those situations into a shape that will fit narrow unifying principles; if we can prioritize place over time without then thinking we must obliterate time; if we can realize that humans are meant to live in relatively small communities strongly connected to places where they remain over long periods of time, and that they are not meant to go wherever they can "make money"; if we can realize that bounded spheres of difference are desirable, so long as the boundaries are more like human skin than fortress walls, we will realize there are tangible, workable solutions to our world problems instead of some sort of postmodern hopelessness.

It is most ironic that these solutions come from the worldviews of American Indians, worldviews recently thought to be romantic, nostalgic remnants of a past certainly useless in the "modern" world. It is also ironic that those people who have suffered what David Stannard describes as the worst genocide the world has ever witnessed would now provide substantial help toward saving those who slaughtered them.

If we can now discuss the worst that has happened in Rwanda, perhaps we can also talk about what has happened here in the United States, for the purpose of unifying our past with a better-imagined future. By participating in this centuries-old American Indian ceremony, and with acceptance of the existence and assistance of American Indian thinkers such as Vine Deloria Jr., we can heal the wounds of our shared past and truly, pragmatically, undertake the role of world leadership to which we aspire.

# Constituting and
# Preserving Self
# through Writing

CONSISTENT WITH THE AUTHENTICITY DEBATE, which seeks to define who is and who is not Indian, individuals who write about themselves have been the topic of much concern. A primary worry has to do with the reliability of the author, based on the assumption that people do not remember events exactly as they occurred. According to Georges Gusdorf, for example, autobiography "does not show us the individual seen from the outside in his visible actions but the person in his inner privacy, not as he was, not as he is, but as he believes and wishes himself to be and to have been." [1]

Gusdorf's statement assumes that events have only single, inherent meanings, rather than several meanings or perhaps no meaning at all, and that meaning is discernible only by certain people. There is the further assumption that the person has no right to see himself as he believes and wishes himself to be. These are examples of Western-style thinking that attempt to establish correspondence with absolute values, or "truths," that attempt to contain "others" as well as the constantly evolving nature of reality. For a writer of American Indian autobiography such as Barney Bush, the application of absolute principles translates quickly into an old colonial agenda concerned with things other than truth: "We

[Indians] are exposed at the earliest ages to colonial America's truths, which are truths only as long as a group of their people have sat, debated, and philosophized long enough to satisfy themselves that this is indeed a *profitable* truth" (emphasis mine).[2]

Concern with potentially valuable territory, such as the "legitimacy" of experience, can be articulated in a number of different ways, one of which is Louis Simpson's recollection: "What was I to think of the new breed of university professors, structuralists, post-structuralists, deconstructionists, who taught that experience had no meaning, that the only reality was language, one word referring to another, one 'sign' to another, with no stop in any kind of truth? Who put the word 'truth' in quotes?"[3] Simpson's remarks, arising from his war experiences, are significant in at least two ways. First, war is probably one of the worst consequences of ideas, as well as the most dramatic illustration of the need to keep ideas grounded in actual experience—those who actually have to fight and die quickly become disenchanted with the idea of war. Second, when ideas are grounded in actual experience, certain "truths" do emerge, and they are usually less transcendental than pragmatic.

For example, Simpson points out that his wartime experience taught him affection for the so-called common man, taught him to value "The life of every day," and most of all taught him his life was his own, to do with as he liked (551–52). Simpson's situation is similar to that of postapocalypse American Indians in many ways, but particularly with regard to dealing with the aftermath of destruction. Believing one's life is one's own is important to survivors of destruction, as is believing that one's experiences have meaning. Within a situation where to live is to suffer, where to survive is to find meaning in life, Indian people often are not as interested in abstractions of experience as they are in making some sort of usable sense of their lives.

Another practical example consists in how many different kinds of information can converge in ways that facilitate interpreting experience into constitution and preservation of identity. Such information often takes the forms of stories and storytelling, about which Leslie Silko says, "you have this constant ongoing process, working on many different levels."[4] She privileges the pragmatic potential of storytelling, dismissing many concerns about when stories are told, or whether they are history, fact, or gossip, as not useful at the present time. In her view, what is important is the "telling," the uninterrupted flow of helpful information sent and received. Similarly, within the postapocalypse situation of American Indians, the fact that a person would presume to tell her own stories often (but not always) becomes less important than making sure they are told.

Many of the less attractive stories about American Indian experiences are usually avoided, or even suppressed. As a result, it is oftentimes left to individuals who have suffered such experiences to tell them. Robert Warrior has pointed out that, "In the concrete materiality of experience, we see both the dysfunctions colonization has created for Indian communities and the various ways Indian people have attempted to endure those dysfunctions."[5] Warrior uses a framework of intellectual sovereignty to illustrate ways to unlock the silenced voices of Indian people who still suffer from genocide. Using autobiography as an example of intellectual sovereignty, Warrior interprets Jimmie Durham's assertion, "I HATE AMERICA," from his essay in the autobiographical collection *I Tell You Now*, as a courageous effort to address greed and violence associated with Indians as well as non-Indians.

Similarly, Warrior describes Wendy Rose's essay from the same collection, "Neon Scars," as being "one of the most courageous pieces of American Indian writing of the last decade" (185). Rose takes confrontation of harsh truths a step further, discussing in excruciating detail being beaten and abandoned by her parents, a confrontation of domestic abuse most American Indian people would rather not talk about. Although Rose's story suggests that many Indian people are still victims of racism, violence, and the process of colonization, it also asserts the particularity of an individual's experience, deconstructing the usual general categories. Finally, and of equal importance, "Neon Scars" forces confrontation of the fact that internal oppressions are among the problems Indian people face. Facing such realities and taking responsibility for them is crucial if Indian people are to reach the next stage of their own critical process, and it is through autobiography that some of the most urgent reminders of this come clear.

It was as a result of these kinds of dynamics that I wrote my autobiography, *Catch Colt*. First, I had always found authority problematic, which I had been taught to believe was the natural consequence of being part-Indian, which equaled bad seed, juvenile delinquent, half-breed, and other negative associations. I did not yet possess the words and concepts to understand that what I really resented was being defined from outside, in ways that conflicted significantly with my own internal discourse. For example, as part of the boarding-school tradition of the early and mid-1900s, I attended school off-reservation in a place that to me was much less attractive than the Fort Belknap Reservation ranch where I was raised. Furthermore, compared to my family, the individuals I met off-reservation seemed sort of pale, so to speak. Unfortunately, I often did not keep my feelings to myself, and when it became clear to certain mainstream individuals that I thought more of the Indians than I did of them, they were outraged. I was constantly being told Indian people were inferior, yet from my own experience I felt strongly they were at least equal and in many cases superior, and that created many internal and external conflicts for me.

As a result of both my bicultural background and my attitude, I experienced much subtle and some not-so-subtle discrimination. Some of the less apparent forms resulted in relatively simple things such as getting jobs and finding a comfort level with day-to-day life being more difficult for me than they were for mainstream individuals whom I observed in similar circumstances. More blatant forms included being singled out for corporal punishment by an elementary school principal and being excluded from prestigious schoolboy activities. Discrimination is complex, and often cloaked in the confusion of authority; furthermore, it is more often than not up to the individual suffering from inequity to deal with it on his own. The ceremony of selecting significant experiences from my life and naming them is so far the most effective means of dealing with problematic experiences of which I am aware, and serves as a useful means of unifying the past and future with the present.

Louis Simpson's recollection of academic devaluation of experience is also familiar. The majority of my mainstream education did not address Indian experiences, a form of constructive devaluation, and perhaps it was for this reason that I found it impossible not to write my own experiences into my doctoral dissertation. Writing my own life into the dissertation met with considerable resistance, and I was counseled a number of times to discontinue the practice. I found it difficult, however, because my own experiences kept bobbing up like corks from under the mainstream material flowing over and around my life. Fortunately, I was eventually able to retain some of the autobiographical material.

Not long after the dissertation was completed, I was contacted by a university press and invited to submit the manuscript for consideration. I did so and received the almost immediate response that the press would be interested in the manuscript if I could subordinate the academic material to the autobiographical stories. The press's reinforcement of my own intuition about the correct focus for my work was ironic, and completely opposite to the university reaction, and was the first time in my life I had been officially encouraged to value my own experiences in such a meaningful way.

A positive consequence of the Vietnam War is understanding and articulation of the concept of post-traumatic stress disorder. Understanding delayed stress reaction is a great step forward, not only for those involved in war, but also for those involved in other violent and destructive experiences such as "ghettoization" and domestic violence. Like Wendy Rose, my mother was subjected to domestic abuse by her common-law husband. My younger brother and I observed our mother being abused when we were young, and I am convinced that has had long-lasting effects on both of us, including a certain amount of floating anger and anxiety, some of which became directed at our mother. In addition, my biological father was not a part of my life, and I never saw him until I tracked him down in my midthirties. I indicated I was interested in having a relationship with him and told him how to get in touch with me. I never heard from him, however, and have wondered from time to time about the elements constituting his decisions about me. On my part, some of the consequences of his decisions have to do with the necessity of undertaking certain aspects of my own parenting, which I think is paralleled by writing my own story.

It is difficult to gauge all the consequences of such unattractive and potentially frustrating experiences, even for those who have been subjected to them firsthand. It is even more difficult for those who have not had such experiences, and as a result many devalue, avoid, and even suppress them. Given the complex nature of negative experiences it is understandable how great the potential is for inappropriate responses, either immediately or after a delay of some time. Again, for me, the most effective means of dealing with negative experiences was writing my autobiography. I then had an opportunity to pick significant events from my life, decide whether they were negative or positive, name them as such, tally the good and the bad, and, most important, feel as though I had gained control of certain events.

The process had some interesting results, including creating a "big picture" of my life that allowed me to see how the positive things far outweighed the negative. In addition, I found myself deciding against being too harsh toward my mother and father, choosing instead to think of them in the context of their own lives instead of as just parental figures. For example, thinking of my mother in the context of being a mixed-blood Indian woman at a time and place when it was not chic to be Indian caused me to realize what a remarkable thing she had done in leaving the reservation and making a life for herself and two children.

Another thing that blossomed quickly was a sense of the tremendous resources provided by my extended family and the physical place of Fort Belknap. My family provided a generous measure of counsel, socialization, and material support throughout the years of my childhood and early adulthood. Because it was substantial and diverse, my family also served as an effective buffer against all kinds of influences. During times of trouble, sorrow, illness, and defeat, as well as joy and triumph, the many levels of family enfolded, absorbed, mediated, supported, and celebrated the highs and lows associated with all our experiences.

Connection to the land is a concept that has seemed romantic and antiquated to me at times, and especially when I was trying to achieve my own independence, staying in one place did not seem useful. I began to understand, however, the deep sense of joy and satisfaction I used to feel upon returning home after the school year. As the familiar features of Fort Belknap's Milk River Valley began to come into view, there was a feeling unlike that of seeing my family again, and I now know that feeling to be a resonation to the land, light, and space of north-central

Montana. To accept that it is possible to have a relationship with a place that is similar to the most meaningful relationships that exist between people is to unlock a treasure chest of meaningful associations.

There is a phenomenon among Indian people that manifests itself in the ways they leave home, often for long periods of time. American Indian intellectuals especially are known for living and working in places far removed from their places of origin, and many of these people assert that their work is helped by being conducted at a remove. At the same time, many also seem to manage to stay connected to their places of origin in extraordinary ways. Writing my autobiography was in part an opportunity to put on paper an internal part of my life that remains strongly connected to north-central Montana. For example, I always gauge where I am in terms of how far it is from the ranch where I grew up. I think and dream and am constantly reminded of those early experiences, and within those senses I am still there.

External forces are undoubtedly partly responsible for cycles of movement and associated thinking, but there are also internal pressures that correspond closely to much older patterns of outward movement, such as hero stories, culminating in returning home after an arduous journey. Writing oneself is a ceremony by which the individual, incorporating internal discourse as well as outside influences, can constitute and preserve such experience, a way of tracking and articulating part of the life of the mind that also helps achieve temporal unification of the past and future with the present.

Sander Gilman observes, "Our awareness of how our lives and times help determine our scholarly questions has been articulated recently in a series of brilliantly written autobiographies. . . . These books are not simply summations of creative lives but rather rethinkings of what life events were important to the scholars and of why these events shaped the choice of scholarly field and subject."[6] This has also been the case with American Indian autobiographies that articulate how individual lives and times help determine important questions.

Autobiography provides important opportunities for grounding representation in some prior reality and for intimate expression of subjective experience, a way of making meaning out of complex reality by a combination of history and narrative. Although autobiography's self-referential connections to the world outside the text have raised questions about verifiable truth, contemporary theorists such as John Paul Eakin have turned from questions of the unreliable narrator to relations between text and reality. These relations explore issues of referentiality related to insistence on a reality external to the text, but to which the text must convincingly refer, as well as how most adequately to connect the genre of autobiography to originally lived experience. Recognizing the complex ways language structures recognition of experience, and recognizing the "self" as a linguistic and cultural construction, Eakin, in his 1992 work *Touching the World*, nonetheless resists conceiving the originating self as unreliable.

A way to begin thinking about the complexity of the interaction of life and text might be to consider autobiography an interactive genre. Interaction might be further conceived as a way to indicate the context of life experiences and to suggest different ways to read translations of life into text. This might enable recognition of autobiographers who see their stories as more representative than personal, an example of a shift in autobiographical treatment from heroic narrative to metonymic lateral identification through relationship.[7]

This shift is illustrated in the way older autobiographies often consisted of a heroic narrative of "making it" in American culture and leaving old ways behind. Increasingly, however, "America" no longer offers one cultural ideal to seek or emulate. American national culture as well as social ideals are splintering into multiple perspectives, wherein writers are creating and negotiating compromises. Such negotiations are an amalgam of cultures and canons bridged by the individual writer's unique perspective.

From Richard Rodriguez's *Hunger of Memory: The Education of Richard Rodriguez*, to Maxine Hong Kingston's *Woman Warrior: Memoirs of a Girlhood among Ghosts*, to N. Scott Momaday's *Names*, the new autobiographers have created various solutions to the violent wrenching from one culture to another that is so much a part of celebrating diversity. Each one, however, practices fidelity to the process of endlessly constructing and deconstructing meanings and selves, a process that is likely one of the more important "truths" they locate.

# Louise Erdrich
## *Protecting and Celebrating Culture*

MY FAMILY OF ORIGIN WAS WITHOUT QUESTION run by women. My grandmother was the head of the family; second in command was Aunt Sis, with my mother and two other aunts lower on the extended-family totem pole, although they governed their own households with comparable authority. Neighboring Fort Belknap Reservation families of midcentury were similarly organized around matriarchs, and when these old ladies—my grandmother, "Aunt Rose" Stevens, "Aunt Julia" Schultz—were alive, they were the only people to whom I ever saw iron-willed Aunt Sis show genuine deference.

My grandmother's power derived in part from the fact that the ranch was on land allotted to her by the federal government under the Dawes Severalty Act, the legislation by which communal Indian lands were converted to private property. In addition, she inherited a sizable herd of the valuable sorrel horses her father, Louis Chambeaux, had bred for sale to the U.S. Army. The story of Chambeaux, a longtime government scout and packer, has been told in A. J. Noyes's book, *The Life of Shambow.*

## Louise Erdrich: Protecting and Celebrating Culture

During my childhood it was clear that my grandmother was the center: we always went to her place about three miles upriver, while she seldom came to ours; it was to her Aunt Sis went for information and advice; she set the tone and pace of life associated with both work and play; and, indeed, she not only seemed to know everything, but was also the most fun to be around. Later, when I sought to return to college after dropping out, it was to my grandmother I turned for help. She listened patiently, then wrote me a check for nearly a thousand dollars, which became a well-known affirmation of education among other family members who had been refused money for other things. When my grandmother died I was so paralyzed with grief all I could do was drive — wandering alone as far as San Francisco before making my way back to Montana nearly a year later.

Aunt Sis was much like my grandmother, although she was even more liberated. When her brothers and new husband were called for duty during World War II, she took over the daily business of running the ranch, then methodically bought out her brothers and sisters. When thieves came in the night, thinking to steal hay from defenseless women, she draped her fake fur coat on my mother's shoulders for padding, then told her where to aim my grandfather's .303 Enfield. The thieves fled when they heard the bullets ricocheting loudly off a boulder near the haystack.

When her husband returned home from naval service, during which he had been sunk by a kamikaze off Okinawa, he wanted to move to Chicago, where he had been trained as a diesel mechanic after boot camp. My aunt stubbornly refused, creating a conflict that was finally resolved when she beat him while he was drunk, telling him she would throw him out or kill him if there was any more drinking or talk of leaving. He settled down, and they became two of the most successful ranchers in the valley.

My mother, Ruth ("Toodles"), a raconteur who could drink most men under the table, and my aunts Dorothy ("Fat"), a rail-thin woman, and Alice ("Rabbit," later transmuted to "Jack"), who as an adolescent announced on a hot August night that if she could not sleep then, by God, nobody else would either, completed a group of powerful women.

All three eventually made lives for themselves outside the reservation, no mean feat for mixed-blood Indian women of the time, dominating, and also financially supporting, their men in the process.

Although these women were not to be trifled with, they were also attractive, personable, loving, kind, and pragmatically supportive. These qualities inspired me to create and teach the American Indian Women Writers course that has been offered by the University of Oregon since my arrival. I always explain that because I was raised by Indian women I feel qualified to teach the course, which I think is the primary reason it has been fun as well as consistently successful. Having discovered the many ways in which Indian women of various regions are different from one another, I also explain that the course focuses on Great Plains women, about whom I feel qualified to talk.

An important part of the women-writers course has been the discovery of excellent fiction and academic writing to supplement my lived experience. Examples include Louise Erdrich's *Love Medicine*, Patricia Albers's and Beatrice Medicine's *Hidden Half: Studies of Plains Indian Women*, Paula Gunn Allen's *Sacred Hoop*, and Annette Jaimes's article (written with Theresa Halsey), "American Indian Women: At the Center of Indigenous Resistance in Contemporary North America." Within this comparison/contrast of lived experience, creative writing, and scholarship, three general observations have emerged. First, and perhaps most important, the situations within which American Indian women find themselves are varied, changing, and cannot be explained entirely by consistent and usually reductionist criteria. Instead, women's experiences are complex and subject to many different contexts related to human society as well as history.

Second, by the Victorian age, European males had created an ideal standard by which women were considered largely ornamental, and with which empowered Indian women were in direct conflict. In order to preserve the Victorian standard, descriptions of American Indian women as being either beasts of burden or sexually lax were created in both fiction and scholarship. Such attempts to change Indian women, however, are more reflective of European ideas of the value of household labor, and of the separation and subordination of domestic life from a public sector, than of any aspect of Indian cultures.

Third, for American Indian women gender cannot be essentialized as an exclusive focus for dealing with critical problems in native communities. This divergence from mainstream feminism exists because Indian women are oppressed not only by their gender but by their class and ethnic status as well. In addition, while it is true that Indian men and women have been impacted in different ways by colonization, most maintain correctly that their problems must be addressed through their united efforts. When Indian women and men do not keep their common interests and goals clearly in mind, serious division and separation is created.

Actual classroom work begins with a discussion of general concepts, all of which orbit around three central issues: recovery of identity, redescription of stereotypes, and resistance to colonization. During this informational phase I emphasize that the primary method for approaching the issues will be each student telling a version of his or her story, then relating that story to those of Indian women encountered in class readings and discussions. Students tell their stories first in a short paper, then by means of oral tradition, in storytelling style. In a final paper, written in deference to contemporary university pedagogy, students are asked to expand on their stories and connections to Indian women.

Exploring connections to Indian women begins with reading Louise Erdrich's *Love Medicine*, a text of wonderful stories about family working in the intersections between oral and written traditions. Discussion of *Love Medicine*, which is assigned immediately as background to the opening general discussion, is deliberately kept slightly off-center by downplaying the usual literary analysis in favor of suggesting the book is much more effective when considered as a model for each student to become better acquainted with his or her extended family.

The next opportunity for connection to Indian women is Paula Gunn Allen's *Sacred Hoop*, which has a shaman-scholar quality with enormous appeal, especially for mainstream students looking for "authentic" Indian experience. Although male students appreciate Allen's revelation of Indian experiences, as well as her perceptions of what is sacred about those experiences, the work resonates most strongly with female students aligned with mainstream feminism. Thus, both genders consistently fail to distinguish the essentialized nature of Allen's analysis.

Allen has much to say about what Indian women can teach about the past, the present, and the future, beginning by pointing out how such teaching has been hindered by the suppression of American Indian women's voices. She comments on the ways woman-centered American Indian traditions focus on "continuance" rather than on "extinction," and how Indian women demonstrate an essential tribal consciousness generating from a tribally inspired metaphysics of gynocracy.[1]

Although Allen is to be commended for pointing out how women have been oppressed, her criticism is ultimately similar to other narrow principles of interpretation, such as the ways some scholars insist on privileging oral tradition to the exclusion of everything else. For example, some Indian intellectuals, such as Wendy Rose and Jimmie Durham, insist that their experiences are different from Allen's notions of Indianness. In fact, both Rose and Durham resist essentialized Indian consciousness by describing how their experiences with family and community dysfunction contradict romanticized notions of Indian people as uniformly kind and loving.

Robert Warrior argues that Allen's focus on female consciousness is ineffective when considered as an end in itself: "In her choice of this I contend, tradition loses the sense of . . . process and materiality . . . the power of tradition becomes a static and impregnable kernel of consciousness rather than a living and dynamic expression of a community. . . . The only goal of such a criticism can be the inward spiral of identifying commonalities that denies the importance of differences."[2] Warrior's comments are insightful, and are made more convincing because they are based in similar criticism conducted by American Indian women.

Jaimes has emphasized that American Indians are not comfortable with feminist analysis or action in reservation or urban areas, citing numerous Indian women denouncing the efforts of Anglo women to define their most pressing problem as male supremacy: "Few acknowledge that real change began to take place only after the tremendous sacrifices of the young [male] warriors of the American Indian Movement. . . . How many [of us] will take the time to send a card or letter to the warriors rotting in prisons . . . don't forget the warriors, we may never see their like again."[3]

## Louise Erdrich: Protecting and Celebrating Culture

Jaimes shifts the focus of Indian problems from male supremacy to white supremacism and colonialism, in which she believes white feminists still participate: "Evidence of the colonialist content of much Euroamerican feminist practice has been advanced, not just at the material level, but in terms of cultural imperialism" (333). From using native ceremonies for their own purposes, to the appropriation and distortion of indigenous traditions concerning homosexuality, Jaimes voices concern about those who would create their own versions of "noble savage" mythology for political purposes. For example, the notion that someone who is gay is thereby a more traditional Indian person, because traditional Indians were commonly homosexual, is absurd, and could eventually cause more divisions among Indians at a point when they are most in need of unity.

Jaimes's criticism of Euramerican feminism is shared by women of other nonwhite sectors of American life. African American and Asian American women, Chicanas, and Latinas agree that white women who dominate feminist discourse have little or no understanding of white supremacy as a racial politic, of the impact of class, or of their own participation in a racist, sexist, capitalist state. By organizing "not merely to fight gender oppression, but also to struggle against racial and cultural oppression, native women can prove instrumental in creating an alternative movement of women in North America, one which is mutually respectful of the rights, needs, cultural particularities, and historical divergences of each sector of its membership . . ." (336). This in turn will be of much greater help in accomplishing the most important agenda of American Indian people: reclamation of land and resources, reassertion of self-government, and recovery of individual identity and social relations.

Feminist solutions offer the possibility of inviting a merging of scholarship and politics that can be helpful in dealing with domination, power, and oppression. However, the positions of feminists, scholars, and other empowered persons can be paradoxical. In the case of women, they are the "other," but as feminists or scholars they remain authoritative speakers who may unwittingly preserve the dominant power relations they aim to overcome. For example, Louise Erdrich's work, which celebrates Indian women, has been subject to American Indian criticism similar to that leveled at those who seek to maintain cultural superiority. Selected examples of Erdrich's writing allow us to explore some of the clash and conversation of modern storytelling, and to decide what is useful in American Indian literary criticism.

VIEWING CERTAIN ASPECTS of American Indian writing as similar to rhetorical synecdoche, as Arnold Krupat suggests, is also a way of observing how modern storytelling works. Rhetorical synecdoche defines stories as being representative of many members of a group rather than personal. However, the blending of a certain degree of personalization into representative stories makes them come alive. This inversion is another storytelling device that illustrates the complexity of contemporary American Indian narrative construction.

Louise Erdrich combines rhetorical synecdoche with personal experience in ways that constitute and preserve Indian culture. Retaining a partially self-referential stance, even without using the first person, Erdrich's redescriptions of historical and family stories make meanings out of heterogeneous, contingent reality, beginning with her own. Much of the value of melding the creation of stories with personal experience is found in the "having-been-there" quality of her point of view.

Erdrich's best work comprises a set of family-style stories based on her experiences with Chippewa culture. "[I]n the light of enormous loss, I must tell the stories of contemporary survivors while protecting and celebrating the cores of cultures left in the wake of the catastrophe."[4] Through her, the stories serve as a surrogate for the oral tradition by which Chippewa people were informed of their individual and collective identities prior to colonization.

Erdrich's first book, *Love Medicine,* reflects a quality of Indianness that has been partially defined by Paula Gunn Allen: "Traditional tribal narratives possess a circular structure, incorporating event within event, piling meaning upon meaning, until the accretion finally results in a story. . . . It is tied to a particular point of view — that of the tribe's tradition — and to a specific idea — that of the ritual tradition and the accompanying perspective that informs the narrative."[5] The native quality of *Love Medicine* is tied to the Chippewa tribe's tradition, which has been altered drastically by Euramerican influences. At this disjuncture between the old and the new Louise Erdrich takes aim, and from it material for many of her stories arises.

Older plains Indian societies depended on large-scale hunting methods, such as the pound-and-cliff drive, that required the participation of every able-bodied person. As a result, everyone was ensured an equal share of meat and hides from which most other manufactures resulted.[6]

Later, horse-and-chase hunting, which favored certain males over women, children, and the elderly, created individual ownership of the kill, shattering the unity associated with collective production and distribution of provisions. Although it was as destructive as it was beneficial, horse-and-chase hunting was short-lived and soon displaced by even more dramatic changes.

During the sweeping changes at the turn of the century all Indians were pauperized, and plains Indian men were dispossessed of nearly all means of fulfilling traditional male roles. As a result, women have assumed almost complete dominance in many plains societies: "In the years after World War II, as more women gained access to steady incomes through welfare or employment, the balance of power in the Sioux household, and in wider community settings, increasingly shifted to women."[7]

This shift of power, one of many adjustments made by plains Indians after the fragmentation of their cultures, is one of the central dynamics reflected in Erdrich's work. Harsh as it is in certain regards, Erdrich's pragmatic view of elements that have changed and evolved in certain Indian communities, and are now understood as part of life, is also rich and suggestive. Although Erdrich's perceptions of change clash at times with structuralist/romantic critics and those who feel her work is not sufficiently politicized, her view is integrated with the functions of tribal society so that contemporary tribal life reflects its own unity.

Erdrich accomplishes this in part by telling of less attractive events, in plain talk that helps "tell the whole story" of native individuals and groups. The more rounded picture that results helps balance preoccupation in American Indian studies with narrow unifying principles such as romanticized notions of Indian behavior that often echo pernicious stereotypes.

This balance is achieved by utilizing such things as inversion, cultural corridor talk, gossip networks, and insider language to texture family stories, allowing the reader to become part of Indian experiences. For example, those familiar with modern Indian cultures read to see how much was left out, while others are given an opportunity to understand the cultures better.

This method can perhaps be further understood by comparison with what Paul Rabinow has called corridor talk, in the domain of gossip networks.[8] Corridor talk is made up of stories that members of groups tell about themselves, stories traditionally obscured by the cloak of fictional treatment. This body of tales can be read to examine how the book's underlying culture has been shaped, a way of making story lines and their characters more understandable.

Further validation of corridor talk and gossip networks exists in Leslie Marmon Silko's essay "Language and Literature from a Pueblo Indian Perspective." She argues that social and vernacular stories should at least get equal billing with other forms such as anthropological collections and the novel. In fact, such storytelling is primary to other forms, emphasizing current family stories and community gossip as essential to the ways Indian people know who they are.[9] Silko deconstructs hierarchical oppositions between high and low languages, insisting family stories and gossip take their place alongside academic discourse.

Another crosscurrent in Erdrich's depiction of modern Indian life is charted by Clifford Geertz's notion of deep-play structures, such as when anthropologists set out to observe people but are themselves observed, which significantly affects the process. Similarly, "objective" observers always bring preconceived notions to their work, which works against objectivity. As *Love Medicine* functions as an observation of Chippewa culture, it also invites readers to reveal attitudes they bring to the text, resulting in a simultaneous backward look, an application of Geertz's idea that "one can start anywhere in a culture's repertoire of forms and end up anywhere else. One only has to learn how to gain access to them."[10] Confusion related to the effects of *Love Medicine* upon readers is probably the most common difficulty with the text, and is caused by these kinds of interplay.

Erdrich's choices of stories and storytelling method are grounded in the context of her mixed-blood background, documented by LaVonne Ruoff: "Born in North Dakota, Erdrich is German on her father's side and Ojibwa on her mother's; both parents worked for a BIA school in Wahpeton. She received a bachelor's degree from Dartmouth College and a master's from Johns Hopkins. Erdrich's maternal grandfather, Pat Gourneau, was for many years tribal chairman of the Turtle Mountain Chippewa Reservation, located near Belcourt, North Dakota." [11] The academic background indicates familiarity with such things as theoretical discourse and scholarly writing. However, the stories from nonacademic Chippewa culture upon which *Love Medicine* is based are Erdrich's most powerful writing.

Current family stories and community gossip are important for the ways they reflect the common experiences of Indian people. Contemporary Indian scholars such as Annette Jaimes contend that Indian intellectuals need to work from a conceptual mode drawn from common experiences of indigenous peoples. Jaimes also urges that American Indian literature be assessed according to this kind of internal criteria rather than by the evaluative methods of mainstream fields. [12]

The characters in *Love Medicine* provide a number of different examples of plain but not-so-simple storytelling, illustrating how Erdrich deconstructs hierarchies among social groupings by helping readers understand Indian people better. The story of June Kashpaw, the backdrop for *Love Medicine*, is perhaps the most dramatic example of the kind of storytelling that can help readers move past stereotypes such as reading June as "the prostitute June, no longer young, who dies walking drunkenly through a snowstorm after a sexual encounter." [13]

Another view is provided by James McKenzie, who says: "Nor is June Kashpaw a prostitute who has idled her days on the main streets of oil boomtowns in North Dakota: . . . The man June has sex with before her death, rather than the 'one last client' . . . is her one last hope for someone 'different.'" McKenzie's conclusion is much more positive and supports the assertion that Erdrich means to treat June and other Indians like her sympathetically, by helping the reader understand her behavior. In fact, June articulates her desire to find a different kind of man, saying about a man she has met, "The eggs were lucky. And he had a good-natured slowness about him that seemed different. He could be different...."[14] Viewed in this light, McKenzie's point is well taken. There is no bargained-for exchange for sex in June's encounter; furthermore, it can be read as suggesting impotence on the part of the mud engineer.

A close reading of the language Erdrich uses to characterize June illustrates that she is not simply portrayed as an ignoble citizen reduced by economic circumstances to a degraded existence. First, she does what she does because she can — she has attributes that allow her a range of movement. Throughout the book it is made clear that June is an attractive woman. Aurelia says, "She sure *was* good looking" (11). Gerry Nanapush reminisces, "Hell on wheels! She was really something . . . so beautiful" (268). June's looks allow her some mobility, and, combined with her sense of independence, they are a considerable resource.

The problem that undercuts June and makes her different from less attractive but more successful characters in the book is her childhood. June is brought to Marie Kashpaw half starved after her mother, Lucille, dies, and she is forced to live in the woods like an animal. Marie says, "But then the two drunk ones told me how the girl had survived — by eating pine sap in the woods. Her mother was my sister, Lucille. She died alone with the girl out in the bush" (63).

The effect of this traumatic experience finally becomes clear to Marie. "I began to understand what she was doing as time went on. It [her mother] was a mother she couldn't trust after what had happened in the woods" (70). As a result, June feels more comfortable with Eli, and eventually goes to live with him for the remainder of her childhood. The issue of trust is never fully resolved for June, however, and it handicaps her.

Lack of trust results in a kind of independence that precludes June from participating fully in family, marriage, or work. Albertine recalls, "She reported drunk for work in dime stores and swaggered out of restaurants where she'd waitressed a week, at the first wisecrack. Sometimes she came back to Gordie and they made the marriage work for a while longer. Then she would leave again" (8).

Although June's independence is one of her greatest assets, it has negative aspects as well. Initially, it places her on the periphery of the valuable support system of family. She rejects Marie's attempt to mother her and returns to the woods to live with Eli. She remains at a distance from her husband, Gordie, never able to fully commit to marriage. Unable to risk the intimacy of motherhood, she makes a better aunt: "Whatever she lacked as a mother, June was a good aunt to have — the kind that spoiled you" (8). In the end, tired of Williston and in no mood to wait for the mud engineer Andy to wake up, accustomed to relying on herself, she walks out into a blizzard and freezes to death.

Although striking out on foot in an isolated area seems irresponsible, June has relied on herself since being abandoned by her mother, so her actions are understandable. Her demise is tragic, but the temptation to explain it simplistically is inappropriate. Through the genre of cultural autobiography Erdrich is able to provide readers with a clearer picture of people such as June, who is more a victim of her mother's alcoholism, in a way that resembles modern notions of child abuse, than simply a ne'er-do-well.

Moving beyond simple moralizing is important not only because it dispels the negative association, but also because devaluing June Kashpaw is an analogue for diminishing the vernacular language that works so well to deconstruct hierarchical oppositions between high and low languages in the book. Better conclusions are found in the ways *Love Medicine* explains the behavior of its characters and provides a kind of storytelling that remains noncanonical, repressed, and devalued in many discussions of literature.

ERDRICH'S *TRACKS* takes place between 1912 and 1919, when the North Dakota Chippewas were coping with the effects of the General Allotment Act of 1887, which divided tribally allotted lands among individual Indians so they could leave their nomadic communal cultures behind and become settled as individual farmers. After the Indian Allotment Act of 1904, each enrolled member of the Turtle Mountain Chippewas born before 1909 received one quarter section of land, with single members of the tribe receiving various lesser amounts depending upon their age. This was part of the transformation of Indian land into

Euramerican property; more significantly, as Mary Jane Schneider has noted in her book *North Dakota Indians,* land allotment had the immediate effect of reducing the total acreage of Indian land by 65 percent.[15] *Tracks* is in part an autopsy of this process, whereby place becomes property, showing how innocent bystanders were affected.

Mixed-blood Indian people occupy a marginal position in an already marginalized culture. In the case of the Turtle Mountain Chippewas of *Tracks,* mixed-blood has its origins in the historical influence of French and English fur traders during the mid–eighteenth century. These traders obtained furs from the Chippewas, who received trade goods in return. This relationship was more than economic, however, and resulted in intermarriage between Frenchmen and Chippewa women. Contact was encouraged by the fur companies as a means of keeping their men content, although most Frenchmen returned to Canada when the fur business declined.[16] The children of these unions were called *bois brûles,* half-breeds, mixed-bloods, or *Métis.*

Another large influence on Indian people was the arrival of European religions in the early 1800s. Julie Maristuen-Rodakowski, in her article "The Turtle Mountain Reservation in North Dakota," has pointed out that European religion came to the Chippewas in 1817, "when residents of the Red River Colony (Winnipeg) wrote to the Bishop of Quebec asking him to send religious leaders to minister to the Indians."[17] Apparently this request resulted from negative aspects of the fur-trade relationship that brought abuse of alcohol and abandonment of Indian women and mixed-blood children. French Catholics responded by establishing schools and convents, accomplished at Turtle Mountain by Father Belcourt in 1885.

In her writing Louise Erdrich points out serious problems associated with the arrival of Catholicism. For example, in *Love Medicine,* Marie leaves a Catholic convent because of physical abuse. Maristuen-Rodakowski states: "Marie later hears that the Sacred Heart Convent is a place for nuns that didn't get along anywhere else, and she finds some solace in that. So much for the ministering of the Roman Catholics, if this is true" (41).

Erdrich's assertion of abuse may seem controversial, but it is consistent with evidence of problems noted by other Indian authors. For example, in James Welch's *Winter in the Blood*, the priest from Harlem, Montana, refuses to bury the narrator's grandmother in the family graveyard. "He never buried Indians in their family graveyards; instead, he made them come to him, to his church, his saints and holy water, his feuding eyes."[18] Welch is my cousin, and we both spent considerable time at our grandparents' ranch on the Fort Belknap Reservation. The perception of negative aspects of Catholicism by both Erdrich and Welch are authenticated for me by stories my grandmother told of drinking and sexual abuse of Gros Ventre females by priests at the St. Paul Mission at Fort Belknap.

The process by which European religion came to northern tribes such as the Chippewas and the Gros Ventres can be further explained by a passage from Sister M. Clare Hartmann's "Significance of the Pipe to the Gros Ventres of Montana":

In 1840 Father De Smet was the first missionary to travel through the country in which the Gros Ventres and Assiniboines lived. Father Point (1846–47) and Father Giorda (1862), both Jesuits, visited them periodically. However, President Grant divided the missionary work with the Indians among various sects. Fort Belknap Reservation, the home of the Gros Ventres, was confined to the Methodists. As none of them ever came to take up their work, the Indians were befriended and taken over by the various Jesuit Fathers. In 1883 Father Eberschweiler came to Helena, Montana. On one of his visits to the Gros Ventres they asked for a resident missionary. In 1885 President Cleveland granted permission for the erection of a mission on the Fort Belknap Agency. Father Eberschweiler took up his abode at the agency.[19]

The zeal with which various religious factions must have prepared for their work is reflected in President Grant's dividing Indian territory for them. The fact that the Gros Ventres' assigned ministers never showed up characterizes their luck at the time.

What makes this process so reminiscent of *Tracks* is that the Gros Ventres asked for a resident missionary because they wished to escape the negative influence of soldiers stationed at Fort Assiniboine near present-day Havre, Montana. Similarly, the Chippewas of *Tracks* are willing to embrace a new religion in return for help in escaping abuses by the fur traders.

Ambivalence and tension resulted from Indian people trying to live with both Native American and Roman Catholic religious beliefs. Knowledge of both was in some ways an advantage, but at other times it was paralyzing because of the contradictory systems. In "Reading between Worlds: Narrativity in the Fiction of Louise Erdrich," Catherine Rainwater states: "In *Tracks*, Erdrich's two narrators likewise struggle with liminality in their efforts to leave behind early lives in favor of others they have chosen. Nanapush grows up Christian in a Jesuit school, but later chooses life in the woods and Chippewa tradition; the other narrator, Pauline, is a mixed-blood raised in the Native American tradition, but she wishes to be white and eventually becomes a fanatical nun, constantly at war with the 'pagans' who had once been her relatives."[20]

Intermarriage with fur traders, although generative in certain situations, was also divisive in at least two powerful ways. Although Indian people were accepting of outsiders on some levels, especially as a way of making advantageous alliances, they still retained a homogeneity at the core of their kinship systems.

In his research on mixed-bloods for his book *Mohave Ethnopsychiatry*, Georges Devereaux points out that the Mohaves have had a cultural fear of aliens, dictating avoidance of all close contact with other tribes and intimate connections with alien races. The white race is considered the most dangerous because of its "acquisitiveness." "The three most intensive forms of physiological interactions — eating, cohabitation, and killing — and the most significant form of psychological interaction — discussing the knowledge acquired in a dream — expose the Mohave to the dangers of foreign contamination."[21]

Within this context, mixed-bloods are considered racially alien, and therefore capable of causing full-blood Mohave Indians to contract "the foreign illness," or "Ahwe," which Mohaves believed could cause death. As a result, mixed-blood infants were sometimes killed; or if they were permitted to survive, their fate was harsh: they were rejected by their maternal kin and shunned by the rest of the tribe. Although this is perhaps more dramatic than the fate of mixed-bloods in *Tracks*, it does suggest the foundations for tribal organizations' strictness with regard to identity.

Mixed-bloods were also considered peripheral to tribal government by traditional members. These traditional members were consistently opposed to giving up tribal land and to the process of assimilation to white culture. As a result, European administrators often turned to the mixed-blood population as a means of gaining enough support to attain concessions; by proclaiming that mixed-bloods could participate in decision making, white agents were often able to achieve their objectives.

In *Mixed-Bloods and Tribal Dissolution: Charles Curtis and the Quest for Indian Identity*, William Unrau documents how Curtis, a mixed-blood Kaw, supported assimilationist policies and allotment. Curtis, an attorney and politician, authored the 1898 Curtis Act, a precursor to the Allotment Act. Although he envisioned the act as a great progressive measure, its ultimate result was tribal destruction.

This devastation was accomplished by giving mixed-blood Kaws voting rights, which they subsequently exercised to overcome traditional views and facilitate allotment of Kaw lands.[22] The exploitation of alienated mixed-bloods represents a primary tension in *Tracks* and is part of the backdrop against which the characters live their lives, which are filled with chaos and confusion.

The book begins with Nanapush's reflections on the state of affairs among the Chippewas of 1912. In his winter count he notes that the survivors of displacement and smallpox fought their way west to exile "in a storm of government papers" only to be stricken again, this time by tuberculosis. He considers the feelings of some Chippewas that the trouble is the result of dissatisfied spirits of the dead, then comes to his own conclusion, "Our trouble came from living, from liquor and the dollar bill. We stumbled toward the government bait, never looking down, never noticing how the land was snatched from under us at every step."[23]

Although Nanapush aims toward present reality with his statement, he is not unaware of the influence of the past. He tells of how Chippewa dead can come to coax the living to go with them, and of how he and Fleur Pillager, a child he has rescued from the tuberculosis epidemic, nearly succumb to their urging. The dead feel it would be better to move on than to live amid the ruin of Indian culture, regarding the living as fools to do so. Nanapush replies:

And we were. Starvation makes fools of anyone. In the past, some had sold their allotment land for one hundred poundweight of flour. Others, who were desperate to hold on, now urged that we get together and buy back our land, or at least pay a tax and refuse the lumbering money that would sweep the marks of our boundaries off the map like a pattern of straws. Many were determined not to allow the hired surveyors, or even our own people, to enter the deepest bush. They spoke of the guides Hat and Many Women, now dead, who had taken the government pay. (8)

With this Erdrich begins to make a more realistic statement about the seeming passivity of Indian people by personalizing their loss of land. As we discussed, the allotment reduced Indian landholdings by 65 percent. Even more significant, which too often goes without saying, when Indian people were coerced into giving up their land, they were at the point of starving to death in an environment that provided few means of survival other than the destroyed hunting culture.

The "bait" that Indian people stumbled toward was meager rations that would enable them to stay alive. Also implicit in the statement, however, is resistance, a determination by some to hold on to the land by the white way of paying money; others take action by calling on the ancient power once possessed by the Pillager Clan, "who knew the secret ways to cure or kill, until their art deserted them" (3). Although some maneuver successfully to retain their land, they are forced to do so as individuals operating largely outside the tribal-kinship system; the overall effect is further diminishment. What seems more empowering in the long run, though less profitable short-term, is Nanapush's and Fleur's adherence to traditional ways.

Although Indian people were promised many times that each land concession would be the last, whites continued to find means for further dispossession. In *Tracks*, although the Anishinabe have been given individual parcels of land by allotment, the land is still being taken away for the people's failure to pay taxes. Nanapush complains, "As you know, I

94

was taught by the Jesuits. . . . I know about law. I know that 'trust' means they can't tax our parcels" (174). What this means within the context of *Tracks* is that although the land was held in trust for Indians by the federal government, the states and others could step in and claim it under certain circumstances.

More specifically, Indian tribes are vulnerable to arguments based on legal doctrines such as statutes of limitation and adverse possession, doctrines that amount to a requirement of "use it or lose it" in various circumstances. During the twilight years from the 1880s to the 1960s, when they were virtually paralyzed by adversity, tribes often failed to exercise rights they would have had commensurate with federal recognition as separate but equal entities. These patterns of "nonuser," in legal parlance, or nonuse by Indians, created powerful equities in governments and private landowners who ruled on or occupied lands more or less by default. It appears that the seizure of land for failure to pay property taxes referred to in *Tracks* stems from this, a practice finally struck down by the Supreme Court in the 1976 Minnesota case *Bryan v. Itasca County*.

In conjunction with this, land was apparently resold at auction after seizure. Nector Kashpaw, in a moment of realization, reiterates: "If we don't pay they'll auction us off! Damien nodded, went on, ignoring Margaret's shocked poke at her knowledgeable son. Edgar Pukwan Jr. and the Agent control the choosing of the board who will decide who may bid on what foreclosed parcels and where" (175).

Erdrich sets up the Morrisseys as an example of those who have profited by buying allotments others have lost to taxes. "They were well-off people, mixed-bloods who profited from acquiring allotments that many old Chippewa did not know how to keep" (63). Excluded from certain aspects of tribal society as they were, mixed-blood people clearly felt that some losses suffered by traditional people represented opportunities. In addition, consistent with the strong matriarchal strain in northern tribes, Bernadette Morrissey is the family leader, and as long as she is in charge they prosper.

This is again similar to James Welch's *Winter in the Blood*, in which the narrator remarks, "We passed Emily Short's fields, which were the best in the valley. They had been leveled by a reclamation crew from the agency. Emily was on the tribal council."[24] In *Tracks*, when Bernadette is faced with adversity, she reacts immediately. "In a week, with her cleanliness, her methodical handwriting, and her way with sums, she had found a way to save her land. In spite of the first consumptive signs in her lungs, Bernadette kept house for the Agent, reorganized his property records, and mailed debt announcements to every Indian in arrears" (179). Bernadette is obviously capable; however, her success is clearly gained in large part at the expense of other Indian people.

Bernadette's success is limited in other ways as well. Like Teresa in *Winter in the Blood*, although she has won the battle to prosper individually, she is losing the war. Her family is in disarray. Her children, Clarence and Sophie, both marry no-account Lazarres and descend on her like a swarm of locusts, whereupon she promptly leaves them on the farm and moves to town.

The significance of family for Indian people has been articulated by Janine Windy Boy-Pease in the 1985 Rattlesnake Productions film *Country Warriors: A Story of the Crow Tribe*. "But you know Crows measure wealth a little differently than non-Indians. . . . Wealth is measured by one's relatedness, one's family, and one's clan. To be alone, that would be abject poverty to a Crow." By isolating herself Bernadette has fallen into the trap of allowing herself to become a shadow of property; consequently she contributes to the colonization of the tribe and is in turn colonized by her own children, who become decadent without her guidance.

Nanapush, representing the traditional Anishinabe, seeks to remain aligned with tribal tradition as much as possible. Although he is made to bend, he does not break, remaining perhaps the most empowered figure throughout the book:

The Captain and then the lumber president, the Agent and at last many of our own, spoke long and hard about a cash agreement. But nothing changed my mind. I've seen too much go by—unturned grass below my feet, and overhead, the great white cranes flung south forever. I know this. Land is the only thing that lasts life to life. Money burns like tinder, flows off like water. And as for government promises, the wind is steadier. I am a holdout, like the Pillagers, although I told the Captain and the Agent what I thought of their papers in good English. I could have written my name, and much more too, in script. I had a Jesuit education in the halls of Saint John before I ran back to the woods and forgot all my prayers. (33)

In fact, much of Nanapush's power derives from language. His narrative is told in the form of a story to Lulu, his adopted daughter. This device is particularly striking to me because it reminds me of my grandmother talking incessantly to me when I was young. She made it a point to tell me in detail things one might think would be lost on a youngster. In order to get me to sit still for this she resorted to things such as making my grandfather saddle up a sawhorse in the kitchen so I would listen while she cooked and talked. I did not think much about it at the time, but I know the value of the stories now. Like Nanapush, someone took the time to tell me who I am, and why, and that is valuable.

Nanapush emphasizes the value of storytelling throughout the book. He tells how he saved his own life during the smallpox epidemic by starting a story: "I fainted, lost breath, so that I could hardly keep moving my lips. But I did continue and recovered. I got well by talking. Death could not get a word in edgewise, grew discouraged, and traveled on" (46). After he rescues Fleur and the spirits of Pillagers come for them, it is talking that revives him again. "My voice rasped at first when I tried to speak, but then, oiled by strong tea, lard and bread, I was off and talking. . . . I began to creak and roll. I gathered speed. I talked both languages in streams that ran alongside each other, over every rock, around every obstacle. The sound of my own voice convinced me I was alive" (7).

Nanapush's verbal ability works on other levels as well. He sees himself as a talker and a hunter and as someone who can wound with jokes. This gives him powerful tools, including rationalization, persuasion, and laughter. He is a ladies' man who casts a verbal spell on Margaret Kashpaw after she comes to his cabin to upbraid him for giving her son love medicine to use on Fleur. He suggests to Margaret at one point that he may have finally lost his virility, and she replies, "As long as your voice works, the other will" (129). There is a recognition of power in Margaret's statement as well as a wonderful evocation of what it can mean to be a person of experience and verbal ability.

Verbal power is shown to have negative possibilites as well. In "Reading between Worlds," Catherine Rainwater observes that Erdrich presents two distinct worldviews in *Tracks*. This is most vividly illustrated through the character of Pauline, who is a Puyat: "The Puyats were known as a quiet family, with little to say. We were mixed-bloods, skinners in the clan for which the name was lost" (14). This is the classic dilemma of the mixed-bloods, people living between cultures and relegated to the lowly position of skinners, drudge work in the hierarchy of hunting society, so unimportant that the clan name has been forgotten.

Nanapush makes his feelings toward Pauline known early on:

But I could not cast the Puyat from my mind. You might not remember what people I'm talking about, the skinners, of whom Pauline was the only trace of those who died and scattered. She was different from the Puyats I remembered, who were always an uncertain people, shy, never leaders in our dances and cures. She was, to my mind, an unknown mixture of ingredients, like pale bannock that sagged or hardened. We never knew what to call her, or where she fit or how to think when she was around. So we tried to ignore her, and that worked as long as she was quiet. But she was different once her mouth opened and she started to wag her tongue. She was worse than a Nanapush, in fact. For while I was careful with my known facts, she was given to improving truth. (38–39)

Pauline is indeed a handful, representing all the pain, rage, and frustration of a person forced to live in two different cultures while being rejected to a large degree by both. Early in the book she pesters her father into sending her to Argus, where she intends to live as a white. Her past reappears almost immediately, however, in the form of Fleur Pillager, who shows up, is raped, then causes Argus to be leveled by a tornado. During the tornado Pauline and her cousin Russell seek safety in an icehouse but are denied entrance by a group of white men already inside. Enraged, Pauline locks the men in, and all but one perish. Overwhelmed by guilt added to her existing identity crisis, Pauline becomes more and more aberrant.

In her confusion Pauline wanders between white and Indian worlds. Initially she assumes a role of keeper of the dead, then increasingly turns to religion. At the same time, she attempts to maintain contact with the reservation. Faced with the distance she has created between herself and the Indian people, however, she grows frustrated and destructive, a caricature of the marginal person. Catherine Rainwater again observes: "Despite her scorn for her Native American upbringing, Pauline (later to become Sister Leopolda) cannot quite escape her old way of construing experience. . . . She recounts the sufferings of St. John of the Cross, St. Catherine, St. Cecelia, and St. Blaise, and says with pride: 'Predictable shapes, these martyrdoms. Mine took a different form.'"[25] This passage helps illuminate what can happen when cultural codes conflict. Pauline's interpretation of experience is presented as dual and irreconcilable; she is not allowed to privilege one religious code or to synthesize the two as a form of resolution. Instead, Pauline is placed in a permanent state of irresolution—she is crazy.

The manifestations of her craziness, fueled by Catholicism, are clearly destructive, as Pauline gradually becomes more fanatic and embattled. In return for a crumb of recognition from Margaret, Pauline tells the story of what happened in Argus, information that Margaret solicits to use against her son's interest in Fleur Pillager. Warming to Eli and Fleur's sexual relationship, Pauline tries to use Sophie Morrissey to get Eli for herself. When Nanapush tries to cure Fleur's waning powers in a sweat-lodge ceremony, Pauline tries her best to interrupt by preaching Christianity.

Although Pauline's portrayal is not as attractive as others that speak to the positive effects of mixed-bloods on the evolution of tribes, it is effective in its detailed presentation of the tragic aspects of such a mixed-blood figure. And, indeed, for every admirable "cultural broker" created by forced acculturation, there are thousands of confused and broken Paulines thrown on the cultural scrap heap; it is important that their loss is not forgotten.

Nanapush has resisted assimilation to white culture to an amazing degree by words. He cajoles, teases, scolds, croons, and prays. In addition, he has used another tribal tradition. He has taken three young people under his wing and taught them traditional ways. Eli has become a hunter able to survive in the woods, although he succumbs to capitalism. Fleur, also a competent hunter, embraces Nanapush's spirituality more fully, although she, too, is eventually beaten down by the loss of her child and the Pillager land at Matchimanito:

She had failed too many times, both to rescue us and save her youngest child, who now slept in the branches of bitter oaks. Her dreams lied, her vision was obscured, her helper slept deep in the lake, and all her Argus money was long spent. Though she traveled through the bush with gunnysacks and her skinning knife, though she worked past her strength, tireless, and the rough shreds piled to our ankles and spilled across the floor, Fleur was a different person than the young woman I had known. She was hesitant in speaking, false in her gestures, anxious to cover her fear. (177)

Although Fleur is temporarily beaten down, she becomes so only after having a powerful influence on those around her. She demonstrates that one's life does not have to center on liquor and the dollar bill, and that there is dignity and even power in such a life. In fact, the circumstances of her defeat are deeply moving; she hitches herself to a cart and leaves rather than succumb to a way of life in which she does not believe.

Eli and certainly Fleur are nothing to be ashamed of, but it is Lulu who proves Nanapush's ultimate triumph. With many of his traditional methods of resistance frustrated, Nanapush moves to Kashpaw land and takes up a position of leadership on the tribal council. From this position he plays his remaining cards and is able to retrieve Lulu from boarding school.

Beset as Nanapush is from within and without, he unerringly turns to kinship ways to work his method of preservation, focusing on Lulu:

You were the last to emerge. You stepped gravely down, round-faced and alert, so tall we hardly knew to pick you out from the others. Your grin was ready and your look was sharp. You tossed your head like a pony, gathering scent. Your braids were cut, your hair in a thick ragged bowl, and your dress was a shabby and smoldering orange, a shameful color like a half-doused flame, visible for miles, that any child who tried to run away from the boarding school was forced to wear. The dress was tight, too small, straining across your shoulders. Your knees were scabbed from the punishment of scrubbing long sidewalks, and knobbed from kneeling hours on broomsticks. But your grin was bold as your mother's, white with anger that vanished when you saw us waiting. . . . (226)

With the return of Lulu, it is clear the saga of the Turtle Mountain Anishinabe is far from over. Nanapush's teaching has taken root, and through this boisterous girl tribal ways will not be forgotten. In *Tracks* we are allowed to ponder lake monsters and ways of existence other than those of the white Anglo-Saxon Protestant and glimpse a part of the beginnings of a new people, the *Métis*, and we are told more about the dispossession of Indian people. The central image of earth, or loss of earth, in *Tracks* proves not only an effective organizational device for the work, but also a vehicle for Erdrich's larger discussion of self, family, community, and place.

Linking *Love Medicine* and *Tracks* is natural, given that they are both similarly rooted in Indian culture. Erdrich's *Beet Queen*, however, was published between the two, and reflects reservation life more as an absence than as a subject of immediate concern. In response to this absence, Leslie Silko, in her review "Here's an Odd Artifact for the Fairy-Tale Shelf," attacks Erdrich for demonstrating ambivalence about her Indian origins, manifested by the failure to tackle political and social problems in favor of highlighting internal psychological conflicts within the characters of *The Beet Queen*.

In response, Susan Perez Castillo asserts, "While I share Silko's concern with these issues, it is possible that some of her differences with Erdrich arise from misunderstandings related to a limited concept of ethnicity and an essentialist, logocentric view of referentiality."[26] Castillo points out the problems that exist with postmodern fiction acting as active accomplice in the creation of an alienated reality. She concludes correctly, however, that such texts can often be seen not only as passive mirrors of reality, but also as space in which two or more distinct worlds are presented. In this regard, the reader is thrust into contact with two widely divergent worlds, namely, that of the oral tradition and that of the sordid reality of post–World War II reservation life.

In *Tracks*, "this ontological flicker between two radically different realities is far more pronounced [than in *The Beet Queen*]. One of the most interesting features of the novel is Erdrich's recourse to a dual nar-

rative perspective, alternating between the viewpoint of the wily old sur-
vivor Nanapush . . . and a young girl called Pauline, whose descent into
madness is hastened by religious fanaticism and a fragmented sense of
cultural identity." [27] While *The Beet Queen* does present reservation life
more as absence than presence, texts are often linked to ideology by
their silences as well as by what they explicitly state; in addition, there
should be no mistaking the political meaning of Erdrich's characterization of the much decorated Chippewa war hero Russell.

I chose to focus on *Love Medicine* and *Tracks* because they deal so
well with family as a historical, unfinished, contested, living organism
rather than because of any disaffection with Erdrich's other texts. It is far
more productive for scholars of American Indian literature to highlight
the relationships between gifted writers such as Leslie Silko and Louise
Erdrich than to concentrate on issues that might divide them: "both describe Native Americans, not as Noble Savage victims or as dying representatives of a lost authenticity, but as tough, compassionate people who
use the vital capacity of discourse to shape — and not merely reflect —
reality." [28]

Robert Warrior, in *Tribal Secrets: Vine Deloria, Jr., John Joseph
Mathews, and the Recovery of American Indian Intellectual Traditions*,
has articulated three central concerns for the development of a new
American Indian criticism: "First, what should the roles of intellectuals
be in the struggle for American Indian freedom? Second, what are the
sources we should use in developing an American Indian criticism? . . .
Third and finally, do any of these approaches allow us to reflect in our
work the actually-lived, contemporary experiences of American Indian
people?" [29]

The third principle of postapocalypse theory is contained in these
three questions, which also point out the central importance of James
Welch's *Indian Lawyer* and Louise Erdrich's *Love Medicine* and *Tracks*.
The third principle of postapocalypse theory holds that the role of in-
tellectuals is to nurture and support those whom they represent, that
American Indian sources should be the primary sources for American
Indian criticism, and that the work of Indian writers should reflect real
experiences. The texts are significant because they are books by and

about American Indians and, most important, reflect the real, lived experiences of Indian people.

The effect on reservation life has been significant. Knowing that others have endured similar problems, and that those problems are not horribly different or unspeakable, or unknowable, is a tremendous relief to Indian people who need to know their struggles with identity, family, abuse, poverty, or addiction are shared by others. In addition, there is a similar effect among mainstream students who read these texts. From *Love Medicine*, Albertine Johnson's description of her relationship with her mother as being similar to a file upon which they sharpened consistently elicits smiles from those who have never been near a reservation. Providing a means by which similarities among people can be emphasized, rather than the usual tendency to reinforce difference, is tremendously unifying.

# James Welch's
## *Indian Lawyer*

THE WAYS IN WHICH AMERICAN INDIAN LITERATURE reflects traditional Indian worldviews, as well as the ways it responds to theoretical frameworks, such as Arnold Krupat's notion of indigenous literature, are varied and complex. In his analysis of N. Scott Momaday's *House Made of Dawn*, Louis Owens says, "What has matured with Momaday is not merely an undeniable facility with the techniques and tropes of modernism, but more significantly the profound awareness of conflicting epistemologies that had been suggested by Mathews and made explicit by McNickle. With Momaday the American Indian novel shows its ability to appropriate the discourse of the privileged center and make it 'bear the burden' of an 'other' world-view." [1]

The melding of mainstream discourse with American Indian worldviews, a tradition started by Momaday, has been carried forward by other American Indian writers, each in his or her own way. One of these writers is James Welch, who began his literary career with *Winter in the Blood*, a recognizably modernist text that also reflected contemporary Gros Ventre and Blackfeet cultures, and has progressed to a head-on unpacking of one of America's most treasured myths in his 1994 book, *Killing Custer.*

Welch's body of work has grown to be rich and varied, but it is perhaps *The Indian Lawyer* (1990) that best captures the natural resistance of American Indians to postmodern schizophrenia, a resistance that has also been misunderstood as a failure to assimilate. Although *The Indian Lawyer* is a competent work of fiction, it is a much better example of resistance and redescription, while employing American Indian and Euramerican storytelling styles. By combining plot, character, and setting with certain devices of oral tradition, such as minimalization, Welch is able to assert a different perspective.

The change of perspective, or of what has been termed *otherness,* is a complex process, as Welch's work reflects, beginning with the positioning of *Winter in the Blood.* Welch's later writing is different in certain ways, moving in the direction of redescribing particular historical, social, and political realities of modern Indian life. Two examples are found in *The Indian Lawyer,* which redescribes relationships between Indian men and white women, and relationships between Indians and the legal system.

The critical reception of *Winter in the Blood* acknowledged elements of the modernist canon, such as an alienated protagonist, fragmented cultural context, experimental narrative, and dependence upon mythic structure, similar to T. S. Eliot's *The Waste Land.* In addition, in 1978, in a special Welch issue of the *American Indian Quarterly,* Peter G. Beidler surveyed the opinions of early reviewers of the novel and reported they "tended to feel that the novel was a negative expression, an exploration of an American Indian wasteland from which no traveller could return." [2] Other interpretations of *Winter in the Blood* focused on structuring devices such as surrealism and distance.

Possibly due to its modernist form, *Winter in the Blood* received much more critical attention than have Welch's later novels. Another important reason for this reception, however, was that the book corresponded closely to the American myth of the "Vanishing Indian." The unnamed narrator, mired in the most basic considerations of survival, is much easier to eulogize than the potent warriors of yesteryear. From this vantage point of relative safety critics have focused on imagery, language, and tone, with but a few addressing the actual lived experiences of American Indian people.[3]

During an interview with William Bevis, Welch has acknowledged exploration of history, sociology, and politics, stating, "Their [plains Indians] relationship to whites is still one of distrust. I've seen it all my life. You know I'm not just guessing—this is observation." Further cultural observation can be found throughout the interview, such as in the context of *Winter in the Blood* and *The Death of Jim Loney*, of which Welch states, "I've chosen to write about these two guys who sort of have self-limiting worlds, who don't try very hard to rise above what they are, because they interest me."[4]

*The Indian Lawyer* shifts even more noticeably away from modernism and toward natural realism than did *The Death of Jim Loney*, while at the same time redescribing the ethnic identity of protagonist Sylvester Yellow Calf. The transformation of Yellow Calf from Vanishing Indian to assertive other is best understood in the context of Welch's larger body of work and evolving critical standards.

Arnold Krupat has discussed how Native American autobiography falls into the category of synecdoche, or seeing stories as representative rather than personal, "and that the preference for synecdochic models of the self has relations to the oral techniques of information transmission typical of Native American culture."[5]

This tendency of Indian writers to conceive of themselves as "a person" under the control of their culture, rather than as an "I" or "Me" in control of culture, lends support to the idea that Welch is a cultural and historical agent. As such, he employs personal experience in the creation of documents informed by a particular culture.[6] This results in a stylistic perspective that might be described as cultural autobiography, retaining a partially self-referential stance, even though point of view may not be strictly articulated as "I" or "Me." This attempt to make meaning out of reality, beginning with the author's own reality, is enhanced by blending cultural documents with personal experience. The result is creation of a "having-been-there" quality attached to the writer's point of view.

The relationship to autobiography is most clear in *Winter in the Blood*, which begins in the first person: "In the tall weeds of the borrow pit, I took a leak and watched the sorrel mare. . . ."[7] It is equally clear, however, that the central character, described by critics as "the narrator," does not relate a connected narrative of the author's life that would cause it to be classified solely as autobiography.

Welch's use of autobiography instead has more to do with utilizing personal experience as a prism through which to create places and individuals modeled on the Fort Belknap area where he spent considerable time during his youth. For example, the cabin in the opening scene is called the Earthboy place. In fact, it strongly resembles the Horn place, still distinguishable by the fenced-in graveyard on a hill behind the cabin, about a mile and a half west of the Cole ranch on U.S. Highway 2. The Milk River behind Teresa's house, the nearby slough, and the sugar-beet factory upriver at the town of Chinook exist as they are described in the book.

Certain characters in *Winter in the Blood* also resemble those who lived at Fort Belknap at the time the book was written. The physical description of Raymond Long Knife (24), for example, resembles a man who worked for ranchers in the Milk River Valley, and often failed to show up for work after payday. Musty refers to more than one overripe character who could usually be found in Harlem at Beany's Tavern (73), named after a proprietor who "beaned" opposing players during a stint as a semipro baseball pitcher.

Although there is less specific detail related to the Fort Belknap Reservation and surrounding towns in Welch's second book, *The Death of Jim Loney*, it still features Kennedy's Bar, the New England Hotel, and Mission Canyon, all actual place-names in the Fort Belknap area.[8] In addition, *The Death of Jim Loney* also contains a noticeable assertion of the "otherness" of American Indian ethnic identity.

Jim Loney is unable to ground himself in his life. More specifically, he is unable to achieve the unification of the past and the future with the present that is necessary to constitute and preserve identity for contemporary Indian people. It is interesting to note that the critical debate associated with the book also fails to achieve such unification, and the resulting framework is largely reduced to the significance of Loney's pursuit of his own death. Although meager, the criticism manages to suggest there is a possible positive element in Loney's suicide, although it seems limited to the ways he controls it. Again there is a strong connection to the construction of the Vanishing Indian.

Although Welch hints at the importance of unifying the past with the present and future in both *Winter in the Blood* and *The Death of Jim Loney*, there is only the barest glimpse of Gros Ventre and Blackfeet history presented through Yellow Calf in *Winter in the Blood*, and the past is completely closed off in *The Death of Jim Loney*. In fact, it is not until his next book, *Fools Crow* (1986), that he fully addresses the past, but he does so in dramatic fashion. In a major departure from modernism, Welch employs historical realism to create a text set in the fullest flowering of Blackfeet culture as the nineteenth century draws to a close.

*Fools Crow* is a delight, combining the best information available from historical sources and chroniclers of Blackfeet culture, such as J. W. Schultz, with a tribal storyteller style that seems to have been waiting for its chance at expression. Welch is at his best in the role of traditional storyteller, drawing harsh lessons from Yellow Kidney's sexual abuse of a Crow female during a raiding party: "I have tried to act honorably. But there in that Crow lodge, in that lodge of death, I had broken one of the simplest decencies by which people live. In fornicating with the dying girl, I had taken her honor, her opportunity to die virtuously. I had taken the path traveled only by the meanest of scavengers. And so Old Man, as he created me, took away my life many times and left me like this, worse than dead, to think of my transgression every day. . . ."[9]

Yellow Kidney's story is powerful, but it is in juxtaposition to the narrative of the demise of larger Blackfeet society that these individual tales become most effective. An example is the story of the Black Patched Moccasins, once a respected band: "We are a leaderless people now. I have tried my best but I do not inspire the young ones to listen. I am too old and I do not possess the strength. Look around you, White Man's Dog, do you see many of our young men? No, they are off hunting for themselves, or drunk with the white man's water, or stealing their horses. They do not bring anything back to their people. There is no center here. That is why we have become such a pitiful sight to you" (97).

Mad Plume's complaint is fleshed out in the person of Fast Horse, Fools Crow's childhood friend, who has joined a group of young militants alienated from the Lone Eaters band and their pacifist leadership: "There was nothing in camp for him anymore, nothing about the life the Lone Eaters lived that appealed to him. The thought of hunting, of accumulating robes, of the constant search for meat seemed pointless to him. There were easier ways of gaining wealth" (193).

These three stories alone contain enough information to come to better conclusions about what actually caused the destruction of plains Indian cultures than that usually proffered. Combined with the retelling of the Baker Massacre, in the context of both Indian and mainstream forces, they represent a significant recovery of the past presented in a way that is understandable to contemporary Indian and mainstream audiences alike. One way such understanding is facilitated is through astute descriptions of human and animal behavior. In the twilight of their tribal existence, the demise of which they fully understand, the Blackfeet people of *Fools Crow* maintain a sharp sense of humor. Similarly, *Fools Crow*'s Raven, who is vain, self-important, and vulnerable to most vices, is also a wise and compassionate advocate for the animal world. Reestablishing contact with the animal world is one of Welch's most brilliant accomplishments and a skill at which he is unrivaled in modern literature.

*Fools Crow* seems to represent Welch's first opportunity to explore his own past—as if, having satisfied the demands of the contemporary literary market, he immediately set to work to fill in the historical gaps in *Winter in the Blood* and *The Death of Jim Loney*. The quality of the resulting work is almost startling, and displaces any concerns about the place of historical realism in contemporary literature. Having accomplished this crucial linkup with the past, Welch makes another about-face, returning to other issues only touched upon in his earlier work.

For example, although he ultimately fails, Jim Loney is successful in the mainstream educational system and is portrayed as being attractive to a professional white woman. His relationship with the white teacher Rhea is important when placed in its proper historical situation. The ethnic image of the bloodthirsty savage was prominent in westward expansion, allowing whites to use rhetoric to transform territorial aggression against Indians into defensive action necessary to save the lives of white women and children and preserve the civilization they embodied. At the same time, many Indian tales considered whether marriage between a white woman and an Indian man — seldom the reverse — might help conjoin civilizations. The answer was usually no, because white women who were captured were seen primarily as defiled; white women who chose to marry Indians clearly had rejected civilization and thus could not legitimately be part of larger Indian-white relations.

At the heart of this kind of Indian story was a gender distinction casting white men as defenders of white women reduced to passive representations of that which was defended. On yet a deeper level, there was a powerful undercurrent of fear of miscegenation between white women and Indian men.[10] Bringing Loney and Rhea together is an assertion both of otherness contrary to the stereotype of the raping Indian male and of the mediating power of women who choose interracial relationships.

In *The Indian Lawyer*, Welch revisits the subject of interracial relationships, moving toward slashing one-dimensional stereotypes directed at Indians in American literature for years, stereotypes such as the noble yet doomed savage and the Indian man poised over a white woman with tomahawk in hand. Underlying these stereotypes is an examination of the transformation from insider to outsider of a member of the Blackfeet tribe. This type of change reflects the central issue of identity in modern native fiction, and Welch's understanding of identity draws on law and social sciences as well as Western literary viewpoints.

To begin, the tension that exists between insiders and outsiders in a variety of situations provides much of the conflict that exists in life and literature, fostering an identity crisis when a member of a group undergoes transformation from insider to outsider status. "To enter this territory is to be confronted with difficult questions. . . . Must one be . . . one-quarter Blackfoot. . . . Must one be raised in a traditional 'Indian'-culture or speak a native language or be on a tribal roll?"[11] In certain situations, such as when we are with family, we are insiders; in many other social settings we are outsiders. This general dialectic becomes greatly intensified when discussed specifically within the postcolonial situation of native people.

For example, at a particularly telling point in *The Indian Lawyer*, Sylvester Yellow Calf, the book's protagonist, reflects that "He had nightmares of waking up in the street, stark naked, alone in a crowd of strangers, not knowing where he was or what had happened, alone and naked and full of loathing of himself, his father, the strangers — and his mother." The passage illustrates the importance of the insider/outsider conflict in the book as well as echoing almost directly David Riesman's study, *The Lonely Crowd*, which "analyzes American society in terms of three stages: 'tradition-directed' (associated with agricultural and nomadic societies), 'inner-directed' (associated with the era of early capitalism when production and mobility ruled social life), and 'other-directed' (inner tuition is replaced by 'an exceptional sensitivity to the actions and wishes of others,' or 'conformism')." [12] Riesman's theory that identity is subject to conflicting forces reflecting the complexity of modern life is apropos to American Indians, who are presently grappling with issues of tradition, colonization, and acculturation.

Malcolm McFee's "The 150% Man, a Product of Blackfeet Acculturation," or his more extensive study, *Modern Blackfeet: Montanans on a Reservation*, provides helpful detail related to the concept of the lonely crowd, a recurring theme in *The Indian Lawyer*.[13] In these works McFee points out how the Blackfeet have become estranged from one another within their own tribe by evolving a system incorporating degrees of acculturation. Within this system there is a white-oriented group, culturally similar to any non-Indian, rural Montana community; an Indian-oriented group, which acts in conformity with attenuated tribal traditions, persisting Indian values, and some borrowed pan-Indian symbols; and the Interpreters, who seek to combine the best of the Indian way with the best of the white way. There are also those who fail to fit into any of the well-defined groups. These elements of modern Blackfeet society correspond closely to Riesman's categories of tradition-directed, inner-directed, and other-directed individuals existing within a larger grouping. In addition, failure to fit into a group, or to be in transition between groups, as is Sylvester Yellow Calf, is to be part of the lonely crowd.

*The Indian Lawyer* uses such concepts from the social sciences in order to move toward a new trend in native fiction, as noted by Alan Velie: "The novels of the past five years, by the same authors, treat a very different class of protagonists: Indian professionals who have achieved a great deal of success and prestige in the white world. It seems that Momaday, Welch, and Erdrich turned from depicting life in the tribal community to a matter that touches them more closely: the question of the cultural identity of an Indian who leaves the tribe to live among whites and becomes so successful he can't go home again."[14] This new direction depicting middle-class protagonists has much value for those interested in how Indians deal with the modern world. Many of these dealings, illustrated in the tribal settings of Welch's earlier novels, feature identity as a central issue.

A survey of opinions regarding James Welch's work can be found in the May 1978 special issue of the *American Indian Quarterly*, Alan R. Velie's *Four American Indian Literary Masters*, and Peter Wild's *James Welch*. Within the criticism are Western literary viewpoints such as comedy, surrealism, and the picaresque hero, as well as comments on Indian references such as the vision quest and hero twins. Consistent throughout, however, is the issue of identity: identity enhanced by a connection to the past in *Winter in the Blood*; identity achievable only by self-destruction in *The Death of Jim Loney*; and identity altered forever by the massacre at Marias River in *Fools Crow*.

James Welch's own comments about his work reflect a central concern with identity. In addition to his concern with individuals who fail to reach their potential, he explores other psychological effects of cultural destruction. About *Fools Crow* he says, "These are really dramatic events, because after the massacre of 1870, the Blackfeet never fought white people again, ever. That was the end — they laid down their arms."[15] These comments reflect Welch's constant vigilance with regard to how successful Indian individuals and groups are at finding viable ways of living, and the consequences when they fail.

Problems related to identity are also central to the haut-bourgeois setting of *The Indian Lawyer*. Riesman and McFee discuss such problems in terms of three powerfully conflicting forces at work within the contemporary native personality: tradition, self, and the direction of others. In *The Indian Lawyer* the reader sees what McFee would call a "white-oriented" Indian who has been brought to the condition of Riesman's notion of other-direction in the most dramatic way. Yellow Calf can be seen in part as an anxious, uncertain conformist, looking for "adjustment" and taking his cues from advertising, the mass media, and politics. As other-directed, Yellow Calf represents the catastrophic shift in Indian character from a person who values family, ceremony, and generosity to a twentieth-century role: he is an employee who finds that his career in the white world has displaced his tribal values. This characterization is in contrast to "older" images drawn through his grandparents, who persist as "Indian-oriented" individuals.

Although little has been written about *The Indian Lawyer*, probably the most thoughtful material is grounded in contemporary social concepts. In "American Indian Literature in the Nineties," Velie says: "The change from lumpen to *haut bourgeois* protagonist represents a shift in focus of the Indian novel from depicting ethnic experience of the tribal group to dealing with problems of personal identity of Indians who have lost or weakened their ties to their tribe because they live their lives primarily among whites." [16] Velie's thesis is that the generation of Indian protagonists following such figures as Abel of *House Made of Dawn*, Tayo of *Ceremony*, and the narrator of *Winter in the Blood* are primarily enmeshed in middle-class white-type problems. Central to those problems is angst associated with success, seemingly more the province of psychology than ceremony.

In his review article "New Warrior, New West: History and Advocacy in James Welch's *The Indian Lawyer*," Robert F. Gish applies social concepts to observe that "through Yellow Calf's political agenda in his aborted candidacy for Congress, Welch advocates the ecological and *social* concerns of a twentieth-century, Montana, Rocky Mountain, New West" (emphasis mine).[17]

The book begins inside Montana State Prison, where James Welch served as a member of the parole board for a number of years. Inmate Jack Harwood, who is awaiting a parole hearing, is doing time for armed robbery, although he doesn't really fit the sociological profile of a convicted felon: "Most of the other inmates were pretty easy to figure out, the patterns were there — poverty, abuse, history of criminality in the family, impulsiveness. But Harwood was something else. He came from a good family, he had a normal childhood, and he hadn't committed a crime until he was twenty-four" (16). The prison psychologist, Larson, suspects Harwood's actions have something to do with power, but neither he nor Harwood is able to fully explain his fascination with crime. In fact, Harwood, too, fits Riesman's analysis of the "little man," a hired employee reduced from hardy individualism and self-motivation to someone who has an unsuccessfully suppressed resentment of power. Moreover, he has no set of beliefs, as in the old days, which might make sense of a life of routine and small calculations.

Sylvester Yellow Calf, the Indian lawyer, is a member of the parole board hearing Harwood's case, and in this role he is part of the social sciences, and a hired employee of the prison system. Although Yellow Calf has become hardened to the work of the parole board, the events of the day haunt him. He has heard the case of Larry Little Dog, whose brother was his childhood friend. On his way home from the prison he thinks about the Little Dog family, orphaned as children and now scattered. The memory upsets him: "A familiar feeling of unease began to wash over Sylvester. He had left so many people behind, so many friends and acquaintances, to live in a world that had little to do with his people" (38). Yellow Calf's uneasiness is consistent with being other-directed, deriving from his feeling of being different, both on- and off-reservation. In addition, his situation is parallel to Harwood's. Although both men share the feeling of being different, neither of them understands it in the beginning. Harwood, however, soon instinctively seeks to manipulate Yellow Calf's alienation as a means of getting out of prison. Yellow Calf, in more relaxed circumstances, has yet to come to grips with all the consequences of being other-directed.

Yellow Calf returns to Helena, where he is scheduled to attend a party with his girlfriend, a white woman. At the party he feels uncomfortable at being recognized as a former basketball star, in contrast to the way he is recognized back on the reservation — as the grandson of elder Mary Bird Walking Woman. Among Indians his grandmother gets more attention for having raised him well. This opposition in cultural values opens up the significance of women in Yellow Calf's life. After the scene describing his grandmother, attention shifts to his girlfriend, Shelley. "She is a good-looking woman, thought Sylvester, warm, gracious, slightly aristocratic. He always felt grateful for her" (49). Yellow Calf's gratitude is a red flag, signifying a feeling of inequality. He does not realize that his gratitude toward Shelley is symptomatic of his other

feelings of inadequacy, one of which surfaces following his conversation
with a political expert who offers him the chance to run for public office:
"Every now and then, particularly in summer storms, the shadows had
frightened him, just as they frightened him now. Only now he was a big
man, a real big man afraid of those shadows and those that lay ahead"
(56–57). In a time of stress, Yellow Calf longs to return to the comfort of
childhood and the care of his grandmother. The danger of this impulse
in his adult life is that he tends to see Shelley as an object of desire, and
as part of a confusing set of problems.

At this point Yellow Calf's discomfort turns into guilt, not unlike
that of Vietnam veterans who agonize over the fact they returned safe
from the war while others did not. He tells Shelley about the Little Dog
family and how he has lost touch with them and others: "Sometimes I
imagine Donny Little Dog—that's the boy I grew up with—standing
just on the other side of that door waiting for it to open again. But it
never will. Not for him. Not for the others I left behind" (58).

As an other-directed person, Yellow Calf has allowed outside influences to provide direction in his life, causing his sense of material well-
being to erode his memories of the oppression of his people. Shelley
reassures Yellow Calf, admonishing him not to hide things from her,
thinking that their communication is as between equals. Yellow Calf,
however, responds in the manner of slave to master: "Yessum. Can we go
home now?" (60). In this scene we also begin to see that Yellow Calf and
Shelley are worried and distrustful but, like so many others, have no tar-
gets on which to focus their feelings.

Another woman enters Yellow Calf's life before he and Shelley
have much of a chance to work out their problems. Patti Ann Harwood
is sent by her husband to seduce Yellow Calf. Patti Ann shares the quality of difference with Jack Harwood and Yellow Calf, and this makes
him vulnerable to her: "After her fourth miscarriage and subsequent
hysterectomy she knew she was not normal. The doctor, the same one
with the hearty laugh, had told her he was tired of dealing with suicidal
women, if she wanted to kill herself she'd have to find a way other than
childbirth now" (73). Patti Ann exhibits the same other-directedness as
Yellow Calf. She allows herself to be manipulated by her husband and
is unable to break free even when he is placed behind bars. Similarly,

Yellow Calf time and again allows himself to be seduced by the white world. Both seek out others to help them resolve their feelings of conflict.

At this point in the story Welch begins to focus on the reasons Yellow Calf is having problems managing his position of consumption and leisure, yet diffuse anxiety, without losing his bearings. Yellow Calf and Shelley go to Chico Hot Springs for the weekend, and he becomes self-absorbed, remembering events of his earlier life. Yellow Calf recalls his high school years, where the narrative's point of view shifts to that of a sportswriter, who observes racism associated with high school basketball. He points out that white basketball fans love to watch the Indian style of play, but when the games end there is no further interchange. Consulting another reporter, the sportswriter is treated to an ugly metaphor: "'It's like being in a monkey cage,' the older man said. 'At first, you're surprised not only that they can perform their tricks but how well they do it. But in the end, you're in a monkey cage and people get mighty uneasy when they're surrounded by monkeys'" (101). The sportswriter's concern turns to interest in Yellow Calf's basketball career. He publishes an article featuring Yellow Calf that alienates the other team members: "Many of your teammates, Sylvester, will have had their brief moment in the sun and will fall by the wayside, perhaps to a life of drink and degradation — so much a part of Indian experience — but you will, must, carry the torch" (103).

Setting Yellow Calf up as a basketball player allows Welch to echo a number of social concerns of modern Indian life. Gary Smith, in *Sports Illustrated*, notes: "Of all the perplexing games that the white man had brought with him — frantic races for diplomas and dollar bills and development — here was the one that the lean, quick men on the reservations could instinctively play. Here was a way to bring pride back to their hollow chests and vacant eyes, some physical means, at last, for poor and undereducated men to re-attain the status they once had gained through hunting and battle." At the same time, "The game that was a highway into mainstream America for black men . . . was a cul-de-sac for red ones." [18] Smith goes on to point out that no Indian has ever played in the NBA and that only one, Don Wetzel of the Blackfeet, has made it as far as an NCAA Division I team (actually, Willie Weeks also played Division I ball at Montana State University in Bozeman), although many have been heavily recruited by various schools across the country. One reason is that Indians play basketball in large part for recognition in their own families and communities, a perpetuation of insider values. They tend not to measure themselves using outside standards such as college or professional status. Playing away from home may become a lonely task, and neither money nor the satisfaction of accomplishment at a higher level of play serves as a sustaining substitute for the adulation of other Indians.

Other Indians, in fact, are essential to the Indian style of basketball in that they make up an off-court team and are as essential to the game as opponents. In an example of the level of community support, the Blackfeet high school team won its first state championship under the coaching of Don Wetzel a few years ago. When the team advanced to the championship game, Indian fans raced home to gather resources to wager, cleaning out the town of Browning, Montana, to the point that the local bank had to close. Being part of such a strongly identified group can be powerful. Attempting to leave such a group, conversely, can also be difficult. Part of being strongly identified has to do with complex, rigid codes of behavior, one of which is that gaining inclusion in one community can provoke exclusion from others.

As Yellow Calf grows apart from his teammates, he turns to two high school faculty members to help him prepare for college. As he starts to become estranged from the larger Blackfeet community, he turns to two other outsiders, Lena Old Horn, a Crow Indian living in Blackfeet country, and Stanley Weintraub, a teacher from back East: "There was a structure among these people that Weintraub did not understand, much less fit into. And so he became fast friends with Lena Old Horn, one of the other outsiders in town. It did not bother Lena that she was an outsider; she had expected it; it would be the same for an outsider on her own reservation. She tried to explain this to Stan, and when it wouldn't sink in, she let it go and did her job at the high school" (107). The ease with which the reader is informed of exclusionary practices among Indian people might seem jarring, but it proves crucial to Welch's exposition of one of Yellow Calf's most deep-seated conflicts, which becomes evident one night when Lena asks Yellow Calf about his parents in front of Weintraub. Yellow Calf is visibly shaken, then tries to laugh it off, but Lena knows she has made a mistake: "She should have known that he was as inwardly timid and vulnerable as any youth who had been abandoned, cast off by those he loved the most. She had seen lots of kids on her own reservation being raised by grandparents, Sylvester seemed different from them, but she knew he wasn't and she should have known better than to ask him about his family in front of an outsider" (109). Yellow Calf was abandoned by both his parents, a cruel disruption of the most basic insider relationship. It does not seem to matter why, or that others stepped in with love: the outrage breeds mistrust in Yellow Calf, leading to a form of self-reliance based on suspicion that colors his subsequent relationships. He distances himself early, before he has graduated from high school: "He had always been a little different—he studied hard, he took care of his grandparents as much as they took care of him, he didn't drink at all, he was always the best athlete even as a little kid—but now without dwelling on it, he knew he had become an outsider to all but the old people" (110). Yellow Calf distances himself so well that by age thirty-seven he is a successful lawyer in a white community. He has suppressed his hurt and anger toward his parents, but as the stakes increase and he finds himself contemplating a serious relationship with a white woman, and being considered as a candidate for Congress, stresses associated with these events begin to take a toll.

Shelley senses Yellow Calf is troubled while they are having dinner at the exclusive Montana Club. Yellow Calf is unsure of the interracial aspect of their relationship, and he projects that onto his decision to run for office. As he continues to probe issues of race, he casts a pall over the evening. Soon he imagines he is being perceived by the other diners as "an Indian free and easy with a lovely blond woman" (122). He thinks of another failed relationship with a woman in law school, avoiding Shelley's question about his decision to run for office. Suddenly realizing the distance between her and Yellow Calf, Shelley also begins to withdraw and the evening ends on a sour note.

Yellow Calf's relationships with his mother and grandmother have made him at the same time wary and appreciative of the attention of women. Faced with the possibility that Shelley will abandon him as his mother did, he seizes the opportunity to create a backup relationship with Patti Ann, choosing to participate in her seduction. Realizing how perilously out of control this act has placed him, he flees to the reservation: "Sylvester had made it with that beautiful woman and now he was running away to the only home he had ever known. Home is where they have to take you in. He had heard that somewhere, but he had never felt the truth of it until now. Until that moment he entered her bedroom, he had been in control, sometimes shakily, of his life. He had managed to keep all the balls in the air, but in the darkness of that bedroom the balls all came tumbling down, bouncing wildly away from him" (157). Yellow Calf's return home is marked by a wonderfully evocative moment when he realizes that his grandmother believes he has not drifted away, but has just been gone for a while. The continuum of their relationship simply resumes where it left off, a tradition-directed phenomenon.

This is not the case with Lena Old Horn, with whom Yellow Calf tries to forge an insider relationship. "She was still an outsider, still a Crow in Blackfeet country, but the people now accepted her in her role" (170). Yellow Calf goes to see Lena, seeking reassurance about his run for Congress. Lena is deferential, in a manner befitting her role. "Let's just say that I'm glad you asked my advice, and yes, I know you will do a good job of it, and leave it at that" (177). In spite of having access to powerful political figures, it is almost exclusively women to whom Yellow Calf turns when he is in trouble, as they provided leadership in the shattered tribal culture of his youth.

Yellow Calf returns to Helena determined to get on with his life, and during this scene he begins to realize that he is dangerously out of control: "There were a lot of inmates down at MSP who had fucked up in situations similar to Sylvester's. He and the other board members and staff always shook their heads in feigned disbelief at such self-destructiveness. Now he wondered if he had been on the board too long, had absorbed too much foolishness. Sylvester drove home very cautiously" (203). Yellow Calf's realization that his position on the parole board is somehow wrong is the first indication he is capable of doing something about his life. He takes a major step after Patti Ann tells him about the blackmail plot. He looks around her shabby apartment and realizes he has much in common with her. "He had gotten his horns trimmed at her expense. And it had almost cost her—and him— dearly" (228).

As part of coming to terms with his treatment of Patti Ann, Yellow Calf also decides to go ahead with his political campaign without using Shelley as part of his introduction into the political world. With this decision, Yellow Calf finally begins to come to terms with the legacy of his parents' abandonment. Both parents were alcoholics, and it is in a skid-row bar that Yellow Calf finally confronts the shame, hate, and fear he feels for both of them. He is essentially a good person, however, and his loathing gives way to an attempt to understand rather than condemn. Drawing on his experience in divorce work, Yellow Calf remembers the people involved as good people, even likable, caught up in forces beyond their control. This allows him to feel empathy for his own parents, and he makes a crucial decision: "He had learned to live with the fact that his parents had abandoned him. He had had a good life with his grandparents and he was proud of them for having raised him up to be a decent human being. He could not be a barfly and he could not hate his parents for whatever weaknesses led them into their lives" (250). This capacity for self-examination, learning, and forgiveness is what separates Yellow Calf from the blackmailers Woody Peters, Robert Fitzgerald, and Jack Harwood. In the end Harwood is "too smart for his own good. It was a game to him, or a challenge, or something. And when it was all done, he let them catch him . . . a self-made loser" (277). The blackmailers escalate their pressure on Yellow Calf to give them money, testing his ability to handle things without turning to the women in his life. He falters in an interchange with Patti Ann, wanting to blame her for the mess they are in, but in the end recovers his resolve: "Sylvester smiled at the pale cupboards. His own anger had passed and he felt a sudden warmth again for this woman. Even under these circumstances, he recognized the frail courage that had drawn him to her in the first place and he wished he could be with her right now. But he couldn't allow himself to feel this way" (282).

The decision not to exclude Patti Ann is a milestone in Yellow Calf's development. He has in one way or another been playing the insider/outsider game since he was born. Although other-direction has largely made him an outsider to his own people, he has a steady, well-paying, and fairly prestigious job. The price of Yellow Calf's success has been considerable, however. He has grown distant from family and friends, and is separated by invisible boundaries from Patti Ann, to whom he feels a real connection. She realizes the impossibility of the situation, having "actually thought of spending a long lovely life with him, but even as she thought that, she knew it would never happen. She would always be on the outside. Later, when she saw him on TV, announcing his candidacy, she almost wept with embarrassment at her foolishness" (301).

There is no easy resolution to *The Indian Lawyer*. Instead there is a recognition of the fault lines in other-directed life and of the hard work necessary to get beyond modern systems that create boundaries. What Yellow Calf achieves is a level of honesty with the women in his life and a step back from elitism, at least for the moment, to work on a water-rights case for another tribe. Although Yellow Calf's work at Standing Rock is perhaps not the kind of homecoming he may have imagined for himself, it has evolved from significant realizations about himself, as he tells Shelley: "You know, when we went to Chico and I couldn't talk to you, couldn't let you in on what I was feeling, it was because I was ashamed of myself. I didn't want you to know that. I felt like an imposter, a poseur, an opportunist who would pay lip service to the issues involved in order to get himself something he hadn't earned. I guess, in some dark but surprisingly decent corner of my mind, I didn't want you involved with that man" (312). There is no clear sense that Yellow Calf has overcome his feelings of inadequacy, and many would say he has not progressed by electing to work on Indian water rights, but he is at least aware of the terrible separation modern life has brought to individuals, families, and communities.

James Welch does not let up on this theme of other-directed separation that helps create insider and outsider roles even at the end of the book. Yellow Calf has not gone "home," either to the reservation or to his life in Helena, but instead has gone away again to a place where he can maybe sort things out. The outsider Weintraub, as baffled by Blackfeet society as Yellow Calf is by that of whites, has simply disappeared. Lena Old Horn, who understands the roles of insider/outsider intimately, is no better off for her understanding and is planning to move as well. *The Indian Lawyer* is the story of a man who has "progressed" in measurable modern ways, but has left behind much of what he needs to be ultimately successful. Because he has allowed himself to become an outsider to family, landscape, and tribal identity, Yellow Calf is poorly equipped to cope with rising challenges. Finally, he begins to learn that he must start over in certain ways.

The loneliness of Yellow Calf's success reflects the fragmentation of the modern world. Until he begins to learn how to deal with elements of modernity such as the celebrity status conferred upon him by the majority society, the athletic fortune that distanced him from his teammates and doomed them to failure, and the law-firm star system that reinforces the idea he is "different," his success leads only to a kind of paralysis.

Yellow Calf's frustration is signified by images of fire and smoke found at the beginning, middle, and end of the novel. Although no fires are immediately threatening, they are out there, smoldering, as are the novel's characters. Yellow Calf, in court, out of court, and on the court, represents all the lonely souls. At the end of the story, however, he travels across the landscape and notices that the mountain fronts are "greening up," the fires having burned out (335).

The message of *The Indian Lawyer*, deriving from the law, social science, tribal values, and literature, is that things are more complicated than they seem, especially with regard to the emergence of the middle-class Indian, a combination as troubling as "Indian Lawyer." This complexity is expressed in the existence of "white-oriented" Indians, "Indian-oriented" Indians, "Interpreters," and those who are lost somewhere in between. It is especially hard to fit into the role of Interpreter, as McFee has pointed out in "The 150% Man," which implies mastery of skills from both Indian and white cultures, and the ability to live in both. Sylvester Yellow Calf is striving to be an Interpreter, although the author does not let him enjoy that role yet. Welch's decision is appropriate, because it is important not to forget the sacrifice necessary to achieve such a position. Many try and fail, and those who do succeed often become much like Riesman's "anxious conformist."

*The Indian Lawyer* takes the reader far beyond the usual rural and urban native communities found in earlier native literature. The concern with identity found in Welch's earlier work, however, ties the book strongly to *Winter in the Blood, The Death of Jim Loney,* and *Fools Crow*. In addition, the narratives contain the hero's journey, totem animals, loss of a twin, and other components of storytelling that coexist with comedy, the picaresque hero, surrealism, and other Western literary conventions. Social science and psychology are also reflected in concepts of tradition-directed, inner-directed, and other-directed individuals, combined with McFee's actual observation of such categories among the Blackfeet. In combination these are all effective aids to comprehending certain native cultures, reflecting at the same time the complexity of what have been for centuries considered simple ways of life.

EXISTING CRITICISM of American Indian literature is primarily based in structuralist and romantic concerns, which is functional to a point. For example, Karl Kroeber has observed that "For effective participation in a storytelling event an audience needs discrete mediative structures that organize the multiplicity of contingent details of which the story treats." It is also thought to be true that the weakness of the structuralist approach is found in its tendency to exclude other aspects of narrative construction. Leaving things out as a storytelling technique, for example, is not valued in structuralist systems, "And the idea of change through reassessment by the audience runs counter to the structuralist focus on the text in itself. . . ."[19]

The water-rights scene at the end of *The Indian Lawyer* is presented in a minimalizing, or leaving-out, fashion that has become typical of Welch's style. Positioned objectively off-center, but with enough facts to carry its meaning, the information is delivered in just one paragraph: "As far as Sylvester could see there were no new wrinkles in either side's arguments; it was simply a matter of convincing the circuit court that the Winters doctrine and later court cases had established that the Indians could protect the amount of water necessary for future and current use. But he read all the pertinent water rights cases affecting Indian property. He knew that each case had to be argued on its own particular merits, that it would have to be argued again and again all the way to the Supreme Court if necessary" (343). The rationale of the case is that neither the Indians in ceding vast land areas, nor Congress in approving the cession, could have intended that tribes would be left with a useless wasteland.

In addition to minimalization, this reference has two other unique features, the first of which concerns the fact that the Winters doctrine stems from *Winters v. United States*, the 1908 Fort Belknap Reservation case ensuring tribes the right to use sufficient water to fulfill the purposes of their reservations. Second, of course, is Welch's strong family ties to the Fort Belknap Reservation.

If there is a worthwhile grail for an Indian hero to pursue, to follow the wasteland analogy, it is certainly water; indeed, perhaps the overriding natural-resource issue in the western United States is the allocation of water rights. The west is semiarid, and cities, farms, and mining interests are applying increasing pressure on water sources. As a result, tribal water codes are coming into conflict with state water laws more frequently, making water-resources management one of the most vital Indian-sovereignty issues today.

The brevity of Welch's use of material from the legal world is effective on a number of levels. Aside from the fact that legal convolutions can be incomprehensible, sparing treatment is consistent with the above-mentioned storytelling device of minimalizing, which causes an active response on the part of the audience, who seek to fill in the gaps with their own imagining or questioning. "The supreme skill of a storyteller is knowing what to leave out." [20]

The reasons for Welch's treatment of American Indian legal issues are more numerous than one might think. To begin, like the strands of autobiography and anthropology, the blend of law and fiction is important to the ways his stories serve as a surrogate for the information passed on to Indian people through oral tradition. Such people are unlikely to read dense academic literature, but many of them read Welch's books, becoming aware of such things as the Baker Massacre, redescribed in *Fools Crow*, and the effect it had on the Blackfeet people, as well as the Winters doctrine and its effect on water rights. From such information Indian and white readers alike have a better chance of understanding key issues in modern Indian lives.

Understanding the effective use of legal materials in fiction begins in awareness of the early years of the American Republic, when lawyers saw themselves as ideological guardians and created strong affinities between law and literature. An understanding of literature was considered essential to proper training in law, even though the synthesis gave way to a narrow professionalism that concentrated on technicalities of the law.

The subordination of literature to law was tempered by early legal thinkers' perception that the popular imagination would exhibit respect for law only if it had proper respect for the history of republican institutions. Therefore, preservation of the present order depended upon the public's perception of the past. It was hoped that through a proper narration of the past a national literature would shape the public's respect for the laws of the present.

One of the most important ways the law actually did fulfill its legitimating function is through its rhetoric. It has been said it was John Marshall's supreme mastery of the existing rhetorical conditions of his time that gave his admittedly partisan results their unassailable quality. The persuasive effect of Marshall's highly praised logic was indebted to his masterly use of the ideological imagery of the law, its use of images and metaphors that helped to convince the public of its impartiality.

Another example exists in what Richard Posner has called the most famous opinion of our most famous judge. Oliver Wendell Holmes, in the 1905 case *Lochner v. New York*, demonstrated how "metaphors, because of their concreteness, vividness, and, when they are good, unexpectedness, are more memorable than their literal equivalents." The *Lochner* decision invalidated a state statute limiting the hours of work in bakeries. In his dissenting opinion, Holmes in effect was voting to uphold a statute he disliked. In so doing he produced one of the most famous sentences in law, advocating sound public policy regarding employment relations through unsound law: "The Fourteenth Amendment does not enact Mr. Herbert Spencer's Social Statics." In brief, Holmes made Spencer's book the metaphor for the philosophy of laissez-faire on the way to writing the greatest judicial opinion of the last hundred years. In Posner's words, "To judge it by 'scientific' standards is to miss the point. It is a rhetorical masterpiece, and evidently rhetoric counts in law; otherwise the dissent in *Lochner* would be forgotten."[21]

We normally consider a judicial opinion to be the product of legal reasoning, but this insight into the inseparability of law and narrative reminds us that the persuasiveness of a decision depends upon an implied narrative that makes its reasoning seem logical. Understanding law in the context of the narratives that give it meaning invites exploration of the cultural narratives that grant the law its authority.

Melville's *Billy Budd* is an example of a story illustrating tension between natural and positive law. John Claggart, petty officer on a British man-of-war, unjustly accuses Billy to the captain of the ship, and Billy responds by striking Claggart dead. Posner points out that "Vere [captain of the ship] refuses to allow the positive law governing naval discipline to be trumped by appeal to the 'higher law' under which Claggart's death was well deserved."[22] The rationale for Vere's decision to execute the popular Billy Budd is based on a British fear of mutiny existing during the war between Britain and the French Directory. Through use of minimalization Melville implies that the decision is justifiable, viewed in light of the considerable responsibility of commanding a ship in wartime.

Legal discourse is aware of its effort to resolve social contradictions but often unconscious of its narrative basis, itself a form of minimalization. Similarly, literature is conscious of its narrativity while often unaware of how its narratives are generated as a response to social contradiction. The tale of a popular sailor killing a hated officer is revealing. Melville creates Captain Vere as a bookish, thoughtful man, implying he can be trusted to make a difficult choice between private feeling and public responsibility.

These relationships between law and literature show how close their social functions are to older kinds of storytelling, such as those described by Claude Lévi-Strauss. Literature's resolutions of social contradictions may be different from those offered by a culture's legal system, but, as Fredric Jameson has argued, a literary narrative often employs minimalization in a "strategy of containment" that disguises or diffuses the social contradictions that helped to generate it in the first place.[23]

The incorporation of law into the narrative of *The Indian Lawyer*, in a manner consistent with older types of storytelling, is fitting, considering that modern Indian people are so closely tied to the American legal system. Again, after much soul-searching, Sylvester Yellow Calf decides to take a leave of absence from his position as partner in a prestigious law firm to work on an Indian water-rights case. His success as a lawyer has been enhanced by a successful lawsuit against a major corporation, and he is a member of the parole board of Montana State Prison. In these ways and others the book has much to do with law.

On the other hand, an "insider" to the legal system might say the book has nothing at all to do with law, that it is only "fiction." This way of interpreting the legal aspect of *The Indian Lawyer* illustrates dogmatic conventional wisdom such as the assumption that law is fact, whereas a novel is fiction; that one deals in truth, whereas the other is fantasy; that lawyers are professionals, whereas writers are artists. In fact, these binaries are too simplistic and serve as an example of the tendency to hide relationships between discourses rather than highlight them.

Highlighting such relationships is accomplished by those who engage in a kind of anthropology, much as literary critics do with literature. Such individuals, for example, might be concerned with Western legal visions and practices as well as forces that challenge the authority and future identity of law. These and other diverse ways of thinking and writing about dynamics of human existence have evolved from processes of participant-observer interaction similar to that of ethnography.

Relational writing is part of a condition of off-centeredness in a world of distinct but related meaning systems, a state of being in culture while looking at culture. This is responsive to aspects of the modern world, such as overlay of traditions, constant movement between cultures, perpetual displacement, and the necessity of being both locally focused and broadly comparative. The resulting strategies of writing and representation are subject to change at such a rate that we can now observe how they become constructed domains of truth, or what James Clifford has termed "serious fictions."[24]

The discourses of oral tradition, literature, anthropology, and law, as historically positioned and locally situated human articulations regarding various people, are all "serious fictions." As such, they are not immutable; their subject matter is radically plural, always open, and there are politics in every account. Most important, as human inventions, these serious fictions are subject to change, which is extremely important to those put at a disadvantage by the oppressive nature of certain constructions.

The view provided in Welch's body of work is integrated with reality as Indian people experience, or have experienced, it, so that modern tribal life reflects its own unity. Welch has accomplished this by first gaining a foothold in American literature with *Winter in the Blood*, an obviously modernist text. Integration with reality is accomplished in another important way, however. Welch creates new layers of story by adding elements of law as well as social relationships.

Welch's use of old and new styles of storytelling allows him to move freely among different devices as a means of constructing narrative. In so doing, he illustrates how the venerable device of minimalizing works, as well as how the metaphors of law are so much more memorable than their literal equivalents. Welch's body of work, especially in texts such as *The Indian Lawyer*, has the potential to correct massive injustices done to American Indians that are only now beginning to enter dialogues of redress. Although there are those doing the good and necessary work of law and social sciences, the more richly textured voice of a writer such as James Welch stands a better chance of making actual progress in the struggle of American Indians to be free.

# Pragmatism
# and American
# Indian Thought

IN HIS BOOK *TRIBAL SECRETS: VINE DELORIA, JR.,* *John Joseph Mathews, and the Recovery of American Indian Intellectual Traditions,* Robert Warrior describes Vine Deloria as being committed to pragmatic politics and being involved in "a search, at once pragmatic and idealistic, for answers to the problems of Native communities and the world as a whole."[1] Pragmatism is similar to plains Indian philosophies that attempt to create a balance between engaging the world as it is encountered and honoring a world of inherited traditions. This sense of balance is particularly valuable in efforts to deal with current problems facing local and world communities.

In 1903 John Dewey, chair of the department of philosophy at the University of Chicago, published an extended discussion of what he named "instrumental logic," more popularly known as pragmatism. Dewey insisted on a precise description of the interaction between the mind and experience, asserting that philosophy was intimately tied to everyday life, and that the philosopher had an obligation to society to use his or her training and ability to help other people. This was different from the Western tradition, within which, from Plato to Hegel, intellectual operations of the mind were thought to reflect some sort of ideal principles of a perfect mind or soul. Dewey's ideas referred to concrete situations in the present environment and dismissed any attempt to establish a correspondence with absolute values.[2]

This basic definition of pragmatism corresponds in recognizable ways to fundamental American Indian notions of family, community, spirituality, and relationship to environment. Such beliefs may be found in texts such as *Black Elk Speaks*, in which sufficient Lakota oral tradition was translated into print to give a glimpse of sophisticated plains Indian history, religion, and ceremony. Although reflective of but one of many Indian cultures, *Black Elk Speaks* is especially useful in comparative discussion because it is one of the better-known Indian stories in America.

Speaking of his visions near the end of his life, Black Elk said: "I recall the great vision you sent me . . . hear me that [my people] may once more go back into the sacred hoop and find the good red road, the shielding tree."[3] Black Elk envisioned two intersecting realities, the spiritual world, which he called the Red Road, and the earthly world, which he called the Black Road, both of which come together at the heart of the world through a flowering tree.

Lakota tradition is rich in content articulated in complex images, yet it remains functional in three important ways. First, the medicine pipe forms the core of a kinship system based on the circle, a unified form promoting balance among all things. All that the Lakota see is in the shape of a hoop, organized into finite divisions such as fourths; for example, four colors, four seasons, four times of day. Additional meanings are organized within these divisions, creating an order that locates the Indian world within a preexisting harmony. For example, the color yellow is associated with the east, where day begins with the yellow sunrise; other stories of beginning might feature an animal transformer such as a light-colored horse as a metaphor for a reminder, lesson, or warning.

Second, the natural world is made sacred by transformations. One important role of transformers has to do with tempering excess, as illustrated by the fact that being "made sacred" often means providing for the black road of material life to be balanced by the red road of spiritual life. In Black Elk's vision such transformation is represented by "interconnected, renewing life forms in overlapping images, from grandfathers who turn into horses that turn into elk, buffalo, and eagle."[4] These images often take the form of helpers, who counsel temperance or warn of danger.

Third, the Lakota social world derives from the natural world. Place-names such as Pine Ridge describe the physical makeup of a particular location; time is pictured seasonally by moons, for example, Moon When the Red Cherries Are Ripe (July) and Moon of the Popping Trees (December); and stories are told in a language of natural signs, as in *Black Elk Speaks*, when Fire Thunder says of the 1867 Wagon Box Fight, "they shot so fast it [sounded] like tearing a blanket" (14). Utilizing the natural world for sources of meaning ties earthly and human worlds together by association. The details contained within Black Elk's story combine to form a powerful narrative, made so by its reflection of complex tribal metaphysics that may prove helpful to serious problems faced by many societies today.

An example of such metaphysics that is emblematic of the majority of American Indian societies is the Iroquois idea of community. Scott L. Pratt has analyzed the early writings of Cadwallader Colden, who asserts that Iroquois society presented human beings as fundamentally part of a community rather than as naturally separate beings: "'Individuals' are defined by their place in the community and are judged by their characters as constructive or destructive in the context of the community. On Colden's view the quality of individuals among the Iroquois is a matter of the esteem in which they are held by others in the community for their actions in support of the community itself."[5]

Colden's view differed significantly from that of other early European thinkers regarding the relationship of individuals to communities. Philosophers such as Thomas Hobbes and John Locke incorporated observations about Native Americans to establish the idea that human persons in the state of nature are fundamentally self-centered.

Pratt's discovery of this particular conflict is part of his larger suggestion that American Indians may have influenced American philosophy, such as in the case of pragmatism. In addition, the study helps illustrate ways academicians are increasingly considering American Indian intellectual history a valuable resource. It seems practical that the mystery and destiny unique to this continent is best understood through its oldest inhabitants, the Indians. It also follows that familiarity with their outlooks, as well as with the history and science written about them, is necessary to any attempt to understand the meaning and character of this destiny. Fortunately, there are well-developed beliefs, such as those of the Lakota and Iroquois, that can help broaden perspectives toward the natural world and human worldviews, especially where those world-views have become dangerously unbalanced.

Lack of balance becomes relevant in light of recent ethnic conflicts. For example, Philip Gourevitch, in a discussion of selfish and violent behavior in Rwanda, compares the country's social, political, and economic structures to criminal syndicates. Gourevitch describes how, from a workable tribal society, prior to German intervention in 1897, Rwanda's postcolonial civil bureaucracy became efficiently organized into pyramids of patron-client relationships, as in what has come to be known as the mafia. This organizational pattern was so rigidly structured that when its chief patron was assassinated, there was nobody else to assume leadership, and Rwandans murdered what is thought to be nearly a million fellow countrymen.

This genocide happened, Gourevitch concludes, because, "far from being part of the failed state syndrome that appears to plague some parts of Africa, Rwanda was too successful as a state."[6] It is ironic that a society can actually be too successful; it is tragic that the Rwandan transformation from a reciprocal and distributive people to worshipers of private ownership and consumption has resulted in mass murder.

A primary vehicle for such transformation is a corresponding violent transformation of reality by language. One outcome of this kind of fundamental disrespect for language is explained by a Rwandan lawyer who said, "He loved the Cartesian, Napoleonic legal system, on which Rwanda's is modeled, but he said that it didn't correspond to Rwandan reality" (93). The Rwandan system is "petty," the lawyer explained, full of chronic liars who tell everyone what they imagine they want to hear in order to maintain their own game and get what they are after.

This situation is representative of one of the most serious difficulties of multiculturalism, where diversity is politically transformed into cultural authenticity that then seeks to become pristine. At this point multiculturalism is quickly reduced to just another form of monoculturalism and provides the rationale for a world always on the verge of dividing into hostile camps. Significant power of imagination is required to construct such powerful prejudice, resentment, and enmity, and "the real question posed by multiculturalism is not how to bring such diverse forms of the imaginary into view . . . [but] how to render them educative or instructive without, at the same time, allowing them to be either hypostatized or coopted, valorized or silenced, in the process."[7]

Pragmatism has been discussed recently as a technique for resisting the application of absolutes to cultural values, having evolved from a method of inquiry associating the meaning of ideas with the effects they are calculated to produce in experience and asserting that all beliefs are confirmed or disconfirmed by whether or not they enhance the rest of our experience. In a world where attention has increasingly turned to the issue of cultural difference, pragmatism has become more concerned with highlighting relationships between discourses and practices rather than reinforcing differences. Giles Gunn has observed how this phenomenon "eventuates in a form of moral bookkeeping designed to show us how to make assets of our liabilities and produces a proverbial wisdom based on the capacity to see the world's vast store of error as a potential repository of truth" (306). This feature of contemporary pragmatism is similar to the negative capability of American Indian post-apocalypse theory.

On the other hand, Gunn admits that incompatibility not only exists but also tends to increase dramatically when placed in ethnically diverse cultural contexts. In the face of such seemingly intractable culture conflicts, pragmatism is no closer to a remedy than any other liberal therapy. In Gunn's view, however, there is a place to start, a crucial beginning that seeks to control the process of scapegoating, wherein we transform others into sacrificial objects for the ritual unburdening of our own unwanted vices. It is especially important that we realize how scapegoating turns cultural essentialism into a mechanism of cultural victimization by not only saddling "the other" with the unassimilated residue of one's own childhood phobias and insecurities but also rendering the cultural "other" virtually opaque to anything it might mediate from beyond itself (308).

Gunn suggests pragmatism might be used to treat the threat of loss by encouraging the ability to mourn, opening new space for the creation of meaning. This work of the imagination, a feature of contemporary pragmatism, echoes postapocalypse theory's second major principle, the absolute necessity of balancing the past and the present with the future.

African American intellectual Cornel West has joined his voice with contemporary pragmatism by suggesting a vocational approach to the life of the mind. West, director of black studies at Harvard University, asserts that such a life should reflect dogged single-mindedness regarding "How to bring more power and pressure to bear on the status quo so as to enhance the life chances of the jobless and homeless, landless and luckless, empower degraded and devalued working people, and increase the quality of life for all."[8] West further suggests the vocational intellectual should seek to fuse the best of the life of the mind from within the academy with the best of the organized forces for greater democracy and freedom from outside the academy. This is a direct reflection of the necessity of linking intellectual work with the living communities on which such work is based, a principle also articulated by postapocalypse theory.

Contemporary pragmatism is similar in these ways to postapocalypse Indian notions of negative capability, redescription through imaginative work, and connection to communities outside the academy. Such pragmatism insists on the value of engaging the world as it is found today, on a level equal with that of the world of inherited presumptions. To do so, we must also disengage from confusing ways of thinking that have blinded us to the full potential of the present moment in its unfolding and infinite possibilities.

An example of disengaging from mystification is found in a recent dialogue between a formerly high-ranking representative of Soviet Russia and an American journalist. When the former head of the Russian KGB was asked if he felt Russia should repent for past injustices, he replied, "If there has to be repentance, then let everyone repent. . . . You should repent for what you've done to the Indians. I haven't heard that from you. If you repent, we will, too."[9] In this instance, face-to-face communication penetrated decades of bewilderment to reveal one of the reasons for Russian distrust of America.

Another instance of pragmatic analysis of dogma is explained in accounts of arguments of so-called revisionists, who claim that the Nazi gas chambers never existed. Ian MacKenzie has observed that while such outrageous beliefs may never be fully understood, they can be clarified and countered, or redescribed, rather than being rationalized as part of the uncontrollably figural nature of language. MacKenzie begins with Paul De Man's conclusion that knowledge is contained in written texts rather than empirical facts and is thus vulnerable to rewriting. The self-fashioned symbols that form the language of knowledge, the primary way of knowing whatever there is to be known, thus exist as what Wallace Stevens called a fiction — a coherent and meaningful, but all-too-human, construction.[10]

MacKenzie continues deemphasis of Enlightenment rationalism by adding Richard Rorty's pragmatic acceptance of the necessity of constant redescriptions of the world. Emphasis is placed on how these redescriptions function, and how they are an effective tool for those who would hope their redescriptions will be taken up by others. Imagination, metaphor, and self-creation, in contrast to rationality and argument, are offered as the most effective methods of redescriptions with potential for cultural change (285). For example, "The major narrative forms of Holocaust texts are the diary, the memoir, the historian's 'factual' text, and the novel" (288). The diary is said to impose the temporal order of hours, days, or weeks; the memoir is contextualized by its ending; and novels of the Holocaust incorporate memoirs as documentary material because of their quality of authority.

MacKenzie undertakes support of autobiographical forms in his argument, pointing out that ideas that selfhood and will need to be eliminated as a means of avoiding gratuitous and irresponsible texts should be subordinated to the value of constituting and preserving self as a moral force through writing. This is emphasized by the strong suggestion that technicalities of argumentation, a strategy used by revisionist historians of the Holocaust, can be overcome by similarly strong redescription stressing "the necessarily narrative nature of understanding and how this determines expression" (291).

MacKenzie's discussion of the significance of stories and how they are told, and his emphasis on imagination rather than reason as the central human faculty, echoes the work of many American Indian writers. An example is found in Leslie Marmon Silko's 1977 novel *Ceremony*:

> I will tell you something about stories,
> [he said]
> They aren't just entertainment.
> Don't be fooled.
> They are all we have, you see,
> all we have to fight off
> illness and death.
>
> You don't have anything
> if you don't have the stories.
>
> Their evil is mighty
> but it can't stand up to our stories.
> So they try to destroy the stories
> let the stories be confused or forgotten.
> They would like that
> They would be happy
> Because we would be defenseless then.
>
> He rubbed his belly.
> I keep them here
> [he said]
> Here, put your hand on it
> See, it is moving.
> There is life here
> for the people.
>
> And in the belly of this story
> the rituals and the ceremony
> are still growing. (2)

The stories of American Indians, more than anything else, have allowed them to survive in the face of such destructive forces as policies of extermination, allotment, and assimilation. Richard Rorty has captured the essence of such survival in his observation that "a talent for speaking differently, rather than for arguing well, is the chief instrument of cultural change." [11] Considering for a moment how well Silko's statement of the issues compares with the "high academese" of MacKenzie, De Man, and Rorty illustrates the point.

Another example is found in American Indian creation stories, which consistently teach that inappropriate behavior such as greed-based violence results in the most dire consequences. From the western-plains tribe known as the Gros Ventre comes this admonition against such improper conduct:

An unknown person, perhaps Nix'ant, became unhappy with the way people were living. He kicked the ground and water came out and covered the earth. All were drowned but The Crow who flew above, and Nix'ant, who floated on buffalo chips with the chief pipe. Crow and Nix'ant became tired of the water, so Nix'ant unwrapped the pipe, which contained copies of all animals. He sent the Large Loon and the Small Loon to dive for mud, but they were unable to bring any to the surface. Then he sent Turtle, who brought up a little earth inside its feet. From this Nix'ant made land. From tears he made water, from the new land he fashioned more people and animals.

[Nix'ant] told the people if they were good there would be no more water and no more fire (Before the water rose the world had been burned; this now is the third life). Then he showed them the rainbow, and told them it was the sign that the earth will not be covered with water again, it means the rain has gone by. He also said there will be another world after this one.

Nix'ant became angry with the early people because they "did not know how to do anything" and "lived like animals," according to the stories contained in Regina Flannery's *Gros Ventres of Montana*.[12]

From the culture of the eastern Iroquois comes a similar story that further clarifies problematic behavior: An intermediary figure in the form of a Sky-Woman arrived to make a dwelling for those who needed it. Animals helped her by diving for earth, or *oeh-da*, then carried her down to it on their wings. She was called Ata-en-sic and was pregnant.

The *oeh-da* grew rapidly and had become an island when Ata-en-sic, hearing voices under her heart, one soft and soothing, the other loud and contentious, knew that her mission to people the island was nearing. To her solitude two lives were coming, one peaceful and patient, the other restless and vicious. The latter, discovering light under the mother's arm, thrust himself through to contentions and strife, while the other entered life for freedom and peace. Foreknowing their powers, each claimed domination and a struggle between them began, Hah-gweh-di-yu claiming the right to beautify the island, while Hah-gweh-da-et-gah was determined to destroy it. Each went his way, and where peace had reigned discord and strife prevailed.[13]

In the Gros Ventre story, generally bad behavior is said to have caused the destruction of the world, and the people are admonished not to repeat their mistakes. In the Iroquois story the definition of bad behavior is spelled out as being devaluation of life: "for any slight offense a man or a woman was killed by his enemy. . . . At night none dared to leave their doorways lest they be struck down by an enemy's club."[14] According to their stories, the Iroquois were eventually able to recover equilibrium when the good brother was able to defeat the bad brother by singing him a song of peace, but overcoming self-interest and violence in order to restore harmony was extremely difficult.

Based on Gros Ventre mythology, it is also possible to define "bad behavior" more closely in relation to plains Indian life, and to correlate that behavior to their present circumstances. For example, it is clear from the creation story above that the Gros Ventres had been warned against certain kinds of actions, which had already resulted in previous penalties of destruction by fire and by water. In addition, Nix'ant says in the story there will be another world after "this one," which can be taken to mean the incarnations of plains cultures before their destruction at the end of the nineteenth century.

It can also be concluded from the creation stories that greed and violence constitute the most serious forms of bad behavior. When these general conclusions are put together with other, more detailed information in existence, it might be thought that abuse of power by plains Indian men after the arrival of the horse, especially toward women and other less powerful tribal members, may have led to the end of the third world. First, as previously discussed, prior to the horse, hunting and gathering required the participation of every able-bodied person, which also created equal status and distribution of the product of the hunt among all. The arrival of the horse favored physically stronger males over women, children, and the less strong by allowing one man to bring down buffalo, aided only by a horse and bow and arrow or gun. This soon created individual ownership of the kill, shattering the unity associated with collective production and distribution of provisions.

Second, individuals such as A. J. Noyes, who, although not extensively knowledgeable about Gros Ventre people of earlier times, are nonetheless considered a reliable source of information from the turn of the nineteenth century. From such information, which Noyes gathered from sources including my great-grandfather, Louis Shambo, a.k.a. Chambeaux, whose wife was a Gros Ventre, it is clear that among those people, "The father was the owner of his children and sold, as a general rule, his daughter to the highest bidder. . . . When the trade was finally made she was taken to the lodge of her husband and began, at once, the arduous duties that the women of the tribes were expected to perform. The drudgery was their part of the contract and the bold husband was to hunt the game. . . . The tanning of hides, the drying of meat, the making of pemican, or the clothes, was done [by women]."[15] This view is to be taken carefully, as it is the source of stereotypes created about Indian women by white men for political purposes; however, a certain amount of documentary evidence exists as well.

In addition to creating a hunter-skinner hierarchy, it also appears there was a certain amount of violence associated with the misuse of women by Indian men. In one story, a young man fell in love with the youngest wife of a wealthy Indian man, and he convinced her to run away with him. The husband hired another man to bring his wife back to him, paying him ten valuable buffalo ponies. When the young woman was returned to her husband, he stood over her and said: "'You are back to my lodge again and you have cost me *ten* buffalo ponies,' and with that remark he shot her, not once, but ten times, a shot for each horse" (11).

Since becoming familiar with certain aspects of plains Indian cultures, especially with changes associated with influences brought by Europeans, such as the horse, I have come to have a strong suspicion it was not defeat by Europeans that brought the cultures down but transgressions against their own moral structures. Furthermore, I believe the Indians were culturally and militarily superior during much of their early interaction with Europeans, and that they were not felled solely by Europeans or by their technology but rather by cosmic disasters visited on them from on high in fulfillment of their creation stories' warnings against greed and abuse of power.

The linchpin of American Indian mythopoeia, as illustrated by these older stories, is excessive devaluation of individual human life in favor of other values. There is a direct comparison that can be made to modern times, wherein individuals worldwide are consistently subordinated to nationalism, capitalism, and other forms of individual and collective egotism in ways that have produced a chronic imbalance.

Examination of contemporary American Indian literature also reveals a strong connection to the past in the form of a pragmatic and humanist authorial personality determined to constitute and preserve American Indian individuals in balance with collective communities. Sophisticated expressions of such equilibrium are found in texts such as N. Scott Momaday's *House Made of Dawn*, which includes a balanced discussion of the nature of good and evil culminating in tangible advice for future action. Abel, the book's protagonist, makes a serious mistake by murdering Fragua, the albino, whom Momaday has described as "an embodiment of evil like Moby Dick, an intelligent malignity."[16] Francisco, Abel's grandfather, knows from his better understanding of Pueblo worldview that evil is to be acknowledged and avoided, the proper way to neutralize its power. Pueblo people view the world as a dangerous place where good and evil, both of which are necessary, exist in a precarious balance. Louis Owens observes that "In this vein, the rattlesnake is respected and feared by the Pueblo peoples and is considered a powerful, dangerous presence, but it is to be acknowledged and avoided, never killed."[17]

Leslie Marmon Silko's *Ceremony*, which builds on the tradition established by *House Made of Dawn*, provides additional ontological information. Pueblo worldview teaches that every individual has immense responsibility for the world that he or she inhabits. Within this worldview there are no politicians, bad parents, or failed relationships to be blamed; each individual has complete responsibility for the survival of all things of the world, animate as well as inanimate, and it is only with acceptance of this responsibility that the individual reaches maturity.

Acceptance of responsibility is closely tied to individual action undertaken to escape the metanarrative of the Western world with its story of separation and ultimate destruction. In *Ceremony*, Tayo, who is thought to be suffering from battle fatigue, is taken to Betonie, a mixed-blood Navajo medicine man. Familiar with more conventional treatments he has experienced in both white and Indian worlds, he is alarmed at the unconventional Betonie, whose hogan is strewn with an odd assortment of telephone books, boxes, and other paraphernalia. He decides to stick it out, however, and by finally taking this personal action he begins to heal.[18]

When the spirit-woman T'seh Montano convinces him to accept her love, and to love in return, he is able to overcome the separation and division Silko describes as being the most powerful tools of witchery and is cured. The lesson about separation and division comes to him as he stands at the mouth of a uranium mine: "they had taken these beautiful rocks from deep within earth and they had laid them in a monstrous design" (246).

These ideas deriving from southwestern Pueblo worldviews are the conceptual equals of any epistemology in existence. For example, the American Indian approach to dealing with evil by avoiding the use of further evil is clearly on a level with notions of defusing the scapegoating that fosters genocide. In addition, such pragmatic and comprehensible solutions seem enormously hopeful in a world often presented as too complicated to understand.

Similar, yet very different, are the worldviews presented by northern-plains writers James Welch and Louise Erdrich. By redescribing stereotypes of Indian men and white women, Indian men and their home communities, and Indian men and the mainstream, Welch's work, especially *The Indian Lawyer*, demonstrates that more than two centuries of serious fictions are subject to revision. By creating a Chippewa-Cree community to rival Faulkner's South, Louise Erdrich has effectively countered the American myth of the Vanishing Indian by telling how

Kashpaws, Morrisseys, Lazarres, and Lamartines have adapted to survive an end of the world.

Perhaps the most striking feature of Welch's and Erdrich's work is how they have faced the American Indian self's continuous need to re-construct itself in the image of the lost past. This process is complicated by the fact that anger, envy, fear, and confusion cause repression that allows the self to pretend the past is still available. Shedding such pretense allows the self to become free to re-create instead whatever elements of the past and future are truly available.

The difficulty associated with such work is dramatically illustrated by juxtaposing two similar, yet different, American Indian voices and traditions. The result is Laguna Pueblo writer Leslie Marmon Silko's criticism of Chippewa-Cree writer Louise Erdrich's work. The resulting clash and conversation illustrates an essential element in the trajectory of modern Indian criticism, that of Indians and non-Indians alike assuming that all Indians are the same. In a review of Erdrich's *Beet Queen*, Silko said: "*The Beet Queen* is a strange artifact, an eloquent example of the political climate in America in 1986. It belongs on the shelf next to the latest report from the United States Civil Rights Commission, which says black men have made tremendous gains in employment and salary. This is the same shelf that holds *The Collected Thoughts of Edwin Meese on First Amendment Rights* and Grimm's *Fairy Tales*."[19] Susan Perez Castillo says Silko's words are "the verbal equivalent of a hand grenade," yet they stem from "a genuine concern about issues related to post-modern fiction and its relation to the real which are of great relevance in the interpretation of Native American texts."[20]

Perez Castillo further comments on matters related to literary theory that bear on Silko's review, but her strongest conclusion comes in observing how much more intact Silko's culture of origin remains than does Erdrich's: "It is also significant that she [Silko] grew up in a tribe which is almost unique in that it has succeeded to a notable degree in maintaining its collective identity while adapting to change. Erdrich, however, is a member of the Chippewa tribe, which for historical and geographic reasons has suffered the effects of acculturation on a far greater scale" (288). Thus, comparison of two of the great written traditions of American Indians demonstrates again the centripetal power of the authenticity debate, for better and for worse, a phenomenon that places it at the center of postapocalypse theory.

In addition to identifying some central features of the postapocalypse situation of American Indians, much critical work remains. First, narrative history written by and about American Indians needs to be reviewed. To continue to avoid truly reckoning with the genocide perpetrated upon the original inhabitants of the Americas is to perpetuate dangerous falsehoods. To accept the Band-Aids offered by superficial legislation and a few token legal decisions as a palliative for such destruction is to become even further deluded.

American Indian fiction needs to be analyzed far beyond the usual structuralist and romantic concerns used to legitimate it for mainstream audiences. It then needs to be placed into current context, and interpreted as part of a coherent body of work. There is a rich vein of American Indian fiction that has done a superb job of recovering important elements of cultures and identities. As suggested by Jack Forbes, however, there has not been a set of criteria generated from that body of work that is also forward-looking in terms of being responsive to the political needs of indigenous people.[21]

Constant attention must be given to the hard questions that need to be addressed concerning the responsibility of Indian intellectuals to indigenous people living less fortunate lives in reservation and urban communities. Within this process special attention needs to be paid to the questions articulated by Robert Warrior: What should the roles of intellectuals be in the struggle for American Indian freedom? What are the sources we should use in developing an American Indian criticism? And do these approaches allow us to reflect in our work the actually lived, contemporary experiences of American Indian people?[22]

Close examination of the issues reveals a number of helpful sources, such as Jonathan Boyarin's *Storm from Paradise*, David Stannard's recapitulation of the genocide perpetrated against American Indians in *American Holocaust*, in addition to the American Indian voices of Vine Deloria Jr., James Welch, and Louise Erdrich. Such examination suggests ways to proceed, as well as illustrating the postapocalyptic nature of the task that lies ahead.

# CONCLUSION

POSTAPOCALYPSE THEORY HAS RESULTED FROM a vast network of tribal nations being subjected to the end of the world in the rememberable past. The discussion related to the genocide perpetrated upon the original inhabitants of the Americas is both absolutely necessary, and crucial to move beyond; it is a primary moving force and the undertow that drags Indian people into a sea of self-hatred time and again. What has come to be known as the American Holocaust is the necessary backboard against which the postapocalypse story of American Indians must be told. However, the means by which the story is told must evolve in ways that can be helpful rather than disintegrating into pointless talk or simply dwelling in the past; while it is crucial that the genocide perpetrated upon American Indians be recognized in a more significant manner, it is equally important to restore to tribal people some reasonable measure of the resources and independence that were taken from them. Such restoration is the necessary first step in transforming the power of unimaginable loss into part of the unification of the past and future with the present.

The discussion of the contemporary circumstances of American Indians might begin with recognition of the similarity of their postapocalypse situation to what has been termed the postmodern condition of all American people. It is generally recognized that World War II was a tremendously unifying force on American culture. During the post–World War II era there was a general trend away from the consensus of the war years to diversity, which has come to be known as modernism. *Postmodernism* is a term that can be used, on a basic level, to represent the continued evolution of diverse thinking that seeks to accommodate awareness of popular culture, minority writers, and general ethnic and regional differences.

In Jonathan Boyarin's view, postmodernism is a critique from within that preserves the freedom of modernism while dismantling its progressivist pretensions to being the last word; it is also characterized by the anthropological stance of participant observation, with emphasis on the insidious potentials of anthropology regarding relations among universalism, imperialism, and genocide.[1] As part of this complex worldview that seeks to engage with the even more complicated nature of reality, unprecedented attitudinal changes are made possible: seeking the right questions to social and environmental problems rather than hasty and simplistic answers; asking anthropologists and other "observers" to reimburse the communities they research; suggesting that it is not enough to remember the past, but that certain things must also be forgotten; updating the ways we presently create social order, the methods by which we ground such order, and of our individual relationships to history.

First, however, it is necessary that human beings make the choices to deal with much more basic behavior, such as killing one another in response to social or environmental perceptions such as protection of wealth and overcrowding. Our most powerful tool, language, is the way such a choice could become part of a psychic conversion away from destructive behavior. Instead, mass murder, for example, is often facilitated by language employed by persons highly invested in agendas who declare themselves to be objective observers, and who then suppress confrontation of the aftermath of genocide by redescribing it. Another example is the way in which certain scholars are puzzled by assertions that the American Holocaust has been "hidden." In fact, it seems to these scholars that the whole canon of Native American literature calls attention to it. Certainly writers such as Sara Winnemucca, D'Arcy

McNickle, and Vine Deloria have all called attention to the American Holocaust, as have mainstream scholars such as David Stannard, in his blunt assertion that "The destruction of the Indians of the Americas was, far and away, the most massive act of genocide in the history of the world."[2]

Such assertions seem clear enough, and also seem invested with considerable power to cause corrective action, yet that has not proved true. In fact, surviving American Indians live under conditions of strictly enforced poverty and continuing genocide, the primary response to which has been demands that Indians forget what happened and assimilate into mainstream culture. Confrontation of the destruction of American Indians has also been deflected by shifting attention to the genocide of European Jewish peoples. Although this kind of avoidance certainly has negative aspects, examination of the politics of memory in the context of the relationship between Indians and Jews can be useful in dealing with various aspects of genocide and its relationship to identity.

Jonathan Boyarin, a scholar working in the intersections of Jewish and American Indian experience, has said that forgetting is a central fact of Jewish life, and an integral part of the loss of "community," of "tradition," and the loss of a "people" by genocide. All these things are considered sacrosanct, but they are also "constructions — and losing them is a construction as well" (7). The observation is helpful, because these constructions are involved in the processes of both forgetting and remembering, and it is important to understand which is operating in a given situation. For example, although a photograph of a place is certainly helpful in remembering it, no photograph can truly re-create any place except in the most superficial way. Similarly, memories are invaluable, so long as it is understood they also tend to omit actual events such as unpleasantries, and to fabricate others. If this is not kept in mind it results in idealization that can create a kind of artificial paradise that leads to extremely destructive behavior when certain individuals are threatened with its loss.

Boyarin uses observations about remembering and forgetting as part of his comparison of Indians and Jews. Although these beginnings have great potential, evidence of the rudimentary nature of his analysis is found in its awkward treatment of political issues: Indians are not so much affected by Christian triumphalism as are Jews; Indians do not have to deal with the murderous cultural divisions of Europe, as do Jews; Indians never achieved central positions in American society, as did Jews in Europe, before being slaughtered; and the Jewish genocide "was both much more concentrated and single-minded and also more recent than that suffered by the pre-Columbian residents of the Americas" (10).

This enumeration of controversial elements of a potential authenticity debate risks establishing irreconcilable differences rather than finding common ground between Jews and Indians, a rhetorical trap to which all analysts are seemingly susceptible. It also, however, contains the potential for negative capability that might help transform genocide into something generative. In fact, acknowledging this primary weakness of the analysis, then turning away from it and highlighting other aspects instead serves as a useful example of negative capability in practice. Choosing to stress negative capability allows emphasis of the way Boyarin illuminates colonizers' universal need to create an illusion that the historical burden of genocide belongs to someone else. The U.S. Holocaust Museum, in Washington, D.C., is an example of how commemorating genocide committed elsewhere serves to draw attention away from the genocidal origins of the United States.

By asking how Native Americans should react to the fact there is a U.S. Holocaust Museum, but no Memorial to the Slaughtered Native Americans, an opportunity for negative capability is created. The appropriate response is not to become caught up in a competition for priority in recognition of genocide nor to assert the sameness of all empires and genocides. Instead, there is much to be learned "through a careful tracing, along back paths not already guarded by the intellectual patrols of neoimperialism, of the border lines where comparative experiences of imperial victimization and resistance meet and separate" (19). The conclusion is strikingly similar to southwestern Pueblo peoples' notion of dealing with evil by acknowledging it, then turning away in a neutral manner. The recognition of similar experiences with evil among different people is empowering as they discover common ground.

Tracing comparative experiences among Indians and Jews has revealed that Americans seem to believe that the past is not of much use: "Indeed, the greater invisibility of genocide in America may be related to the general devaluation of history here compared to Europe" (29–30). This also reveals the danger of oppressed people defining themselves too closely through their subjection to genocide, which interferes with internally differentiated definitions and a range of autonomous linkages to other peoples. Being aware of this is not only a way of avoiding "acceding to the mythified uniqueness of the Jewish genocide, a la Elie Wiesel and the President's Holocaust Commission," but is also a way to highlight relationships (111).

From yet another angle of vision, Jews have been useful to Christian Europe as a lesson in the degradation of the unredeemed soul, as well as being considered dispensable when the idea of individual redemption gave way to that of collective progress through an earthly nation-state. American Indians might be able to observe a comparable critical trajectory: "first, the connection in North American settler ideology between collective expansion and individual sedentarism; second, the presumption that all Indians were alike, and thus could be indefinitely shifted further toward the 'underused' west without harm to themselves or each other; and third, the idea the only hope for Native Americans to survive was as individual Christians" (19). Sorting out the confusion resulting from manipulation of the relationships between religious beliefs, power, and landscape might be helpful in understanding why people are killing each other at an ever increasing rate.

Comparison study of Jewish and Indian peoples also aids in mapping other useful actions with regard to the issue of genocide. First, such study generates conversation that deconstructs the assumed authority of any nation-state to enforce silence, or to deny the issue standing, which is the legal term for agreeing that discussion of a problem can begin. Second, such a conversation precludes shifting the historical burden of genocide from those responsible to someone else, or to some other issue. An example is encouraging debates about which group is entitled to claim the word *Holocaust* as their own cultural currency. When these various forms of avoidance and denial give way to a process of healing, the necessary work of understanding and preventing future destructive behavior can begin.

Although dealing with genocide is of first priority for American Indians, because it is so closely tied to foundational behavior upon which

other considerations depend, there are other matters that figure prominently in any kind of effective unification of the past and future with the
present. The psychic conversion of majority culture from concern with
universal individual spiritual redemption to a territorial, earthly dream
of collective progress through a well-defined nation-state produces dramatic changes in all cultures and demands further examination. A modern consequence of the resulting sense of place has been articulated:
"geography is a product of and a resource in the struggle of groups of
people to attain legitimacy and power simultaneously — that is, to make
and establish themselves as nations" (117). This conception of place is
different from American Indian ideas, such as those of Vine Deloria Jr.

The phrase "the earth is our mother" has become associated with
American Indian people to the point of stereotype, and, like all stereotypes, its actual workings have great potential for misunderstanding. Deloria says, "At the deepest philosophical level our universe must have as
a structure a set of relationships in which all entities participate. Within
the physical world this universal structure can best be understood as a
recognition of the sacredness of places."[3] The statement leads to Deloria's comparative discussion of religion, wherein Jewish people figure
prominently.

Deloria suggests that different societies recall in their religious traditions various geographical histories of the planet, stating, "it is with the
emergence of the Hebrews as a migrating nation into Canaan that the
community and the land merge into a psychic and religious unity. From
that time on the people orient themselves around the idea that God has
given them this particular piece of land" (144). In the Jewish context, that
piece of land was Palestine, the loss of which is still a central dynamic of
their culture. From the time of the Romans, dealing with Jewish fanaticism about restoration of landownership has been a major concern, including the Christian attempt to eliminate the dimension of land from
religion by substituting the concept of *heaven*.

It is possible that all peoples' social organizations are founded on
the lands on which the people reside. For example, the religion of Indian
people remains strongly based on this concept, symbolized by the importance of living on the dust of their ancestors' bones. This in turn is a
reflection of two basic themes: that the earth is alive, and that it conse-

crates human activities. In fact, these two themes encapsulate the meaning of the relationship between lands, spiritual energies, and peoples. As Deloria points out: "Land [has] an unsuspected spiritual energy or identity that shapes and directs human activities. Religions must not be simple expressions of ethical and moral codes as we have been taught. They must be more complicated manifestations of the living earth itself and this aspect of religion is something that American Indians of all the peoples on earth represented" (148).

The importance of land is also present in Western worldviews, but has transmuted into various forms of patriotism and religious nationalism. For example, the emphasis on Rome as the center of Christendom and of Jerusalem as the Hebrew center in European theology has to do primarily with a physical location, rather than with a place invested with sacred beliefs, a disruption of the relationship between religion and land. Yet, the religious dimension of land is a factor that cannot be neglected.

For example, it has been suggested that Christianity has never been able to fully contain older spirits, including the fierce Teutonic gods of Germany and the ghosts of England. Deloria notes, "Jung said that he could see in the psychological problems of his German patients the symbols of the old Germanic religious myths that were to later mark part of the development of Nazi fanaticism among the young" (147). This kind of religious symbolism and its correspondence with the land, and the lack of a universal symbol system of religious experience, have led to much of the current social, political, and military conflict among people. Although some, like Northrop Frye, have attempted such work, the lack of acknowledgment of a common denominator such as connection to land masses has proven problematic. Progress has also been slowed by fragmenting nationalisms, an example of which can actually be found in Frye's work, wherein his considerable progress toward establishing a universal symbol system of religious experience was essentially disrupted by deconstruction, the primary legacy of which has been creation of a sense of literary criticism as a dialogue among critics only.

Understanding the relation of symbol systems to landscape is complicated by other intervening concepts as well, some of which bear serious consideration. In Boyarin's view, the spiritual connection to land advocated by Deloria is seriously problematic. Boyarin describes an obsessive tendency toward spatial categorization in ethnography, and a linkage between ethnographic spatialism and imperial politics, leading to "The denial of history—of a chronological, developmental dimension—to the natives of North America, along with the denial of their proprietary rights. . . . The United States 'was defined primarily as a place'" (59). This critique of spatialism, or of land-based perceptions, leads to the prejudice that Europeans exist in time, in history, while those people studied by anthropology exist only in culture, space, place, and geography, all of which are perceived as being roughly the same thing.

The critique leads to an interesting comparison with Jewish people, whose collective identity is described as being inconsistent with ethnographic spatialism, an expansion of ideas related to connection to place, or land. Although individual Jewish people may be strongly grounded in the places where they live, their collective, or "national," existence is associated more with Israel, a place where few actually live. This is an example of the meaning of "the politics of memory" in practice, where it is important to realize that both remembering and forgetting may be operational—there is a sense of loss of homeland, with implied issues of forgetting, that accompanies remembering Jewish identity. For Jews situated away from Israel, "This dwelling in loss, rather than in a richly detailed space reconstituted through memory, is another term for . . . 'deterritorialization' . . . an overcoming of the fixation on the metaphor of roots" (97). In fact, Boyarin concludes his book by calling for a move away from grounding collective identity in exclusivist territoriality, which has tremendous implications for American Indian people: "In fact, recognizing this tension between local identity and 'historical memory' . . . can illuminate the different possible groundings of various Jewish communities and bring home the point that the spatial factor, far from being irrelevant to Jewish culture, is both necessary and inseparable from time. Yet even when Jews do live on their 'own' land, the collective is today still defined genealogically rather than territorially: Israel's Arab citizens are usually excluded from the common understanding of 'Israeli' identity" (62). Recognition of the tension between local identity, historical memory, and situation of place addresses certain vital circumstances of urban Indian people also, people who live apart from the places that represent the remains of their homelands, and who are without question the most underrepresented group within American Indian cultures and scholarship.

Although urban Indian people do not live on reservations, the equivalent of living apart from Israel for Jewish people, they still identify strongly as Indians, creating tremendous conflict because of the failure of reservation Indians to update their practice of grounding collective identity in exclusivist territoriality. Such updating could be accomplished by balancing connection to place with more recognition of history as the atmosphere we must all breathe and share. Raising to equal status those Indian people who associate with tribal cultures through memories, symbolic representations, and occasional visits with those who live on ancestral homelands would be an incredibly unifying action for American Indians. This is also an example of an actual application of postapocalypse theory that can serve as a means of critique from within that preserves the freedom of the contemporary situation, while dismantling any pretension that there is no need for change.

An equally useful action that would further mediate grounding collective identity in exclusivist territoriality is to redescribe the situation within which many American Indian intellectuals find themselves. For various reasons, many of these individuals live at great distance from the places where they were raised, and from their genealogical roots. Boyarin writes of such a person, Edmond Jabes, who identifies as a Jew while remaining removed from the Jewish community. In discussing the pros and cons of such positioning, Derrida's suggestion that in order to attain vision we must be separated from life and communities is brought into play: once having lost the ideal of organic community (the garden), "the only way we can learn to 'see' is by [separation]" (68).

Deconstruction of the authenticity of grounding identity in exclusivist territoriality has produced the wonderful image of the textual home where landless Israelites live, as well as the concept of refusing to declare the oral word prior to the written (71). Although it is not necessary to devalue American Indian oral tradition, this area could use updating as well, and the example that comes to mind is scholarly emphasis on oral materials that have contributed in some cases to narrow principles of interpretation in American Indian literary criticism. Finding ways to avoid penalizing Indian people who do not have access to materials and language of the oral tradition, such as urban Indians, is one way change could help foster unity.

American Indians, like everyone, have a great need of dealing effectively with loss. Boyarin suggests the importance of memory to this process, describing three types of collective loss: the loss of space, the loss of tradition, and the actual loss of people via genocide: "The loss of a particular space, of a face-to-face everyday 'community' of those sharing a common culture, is [one of] three concentric registers of collective loss" (7). This consideration seems especially appropriate for urban Indians, who become triply marginalized by living on the fringes of mainstream cities. Naming the loss of space resulting in being crowded into urban ghettos would likely be helpful to those who lack the means of understanding the mediative structures that cause many of their contemporary problems.

Part of the process of understanding is the notion embedded in Boyarin's understanding of collective loss: "Much as these forms of loss, especially the last (genocide), appear sacrosanct, I intend to emphasize here, by placing them within quotation marks, that they are indeed constructions — and losing them is a construction as well" (7). One implication of his statement is that, for all people, while it is crucial to remember certain things, it is equally imperative to forget others, and to understand the workings of both remembering and forgetting. Although these kinds of comparisons need to be made carefully, they have great potential. As Franz Kafka has said: "What makes [writing] so powerfully evocative is not that it *restores* a lost world to our vision, but precisely that it can remind us that we are not the first generation to find that loss is the heart of our connection" (97).

Walter Benjamin has suggested that nostalgia tends to opportunistically fill the need for an image of the past that can no longer be provided by older techniques such as storytelling. Benjamin's observation suggests the utility of finding a poetics of memory that fills the need for an image of the past, but that also helps awaken us to the need to balance the hold of the past with considerations of the future. This echoes the need for unification of the past and future with the present as articulated by postapocalypse theory, and, without denigrating in any way the losses suffered by American Indians, also illustrates how the concept of negative capability can be applied even to situations of extreme atrocity.

The search for a useful poetics of memory can also be found in American Indian literature and associated literary criticism. American Indian writers have done well at the task of producing a body of creative work that cultivates many of the intersections of their interaction with tradition and contemporary experiences. The task of secondary criticism, however, has remained largely the province of mainstream writers applying the criteria of mainstream scholarship. As a result, an immediate need of the American Indian intellectual community is to add to the body of contemporary critical work begun by writers such as Kenneth Lincoln, Louis Owens, and Robert Allen Warrior, and to continue to create and apply criteria generated from tribal worldviews.

Through the development of such things as new criticism and modernism, mainstream literary criticism attempted to shift the focus of existence out of the context of culture and into the literary text. One of the results of this effort was a suppression of lived experience that produced a scarcity of writers of the caliber of a Joyce, or a Pound, or a Stevens to truly challenge critics. This situation, wherein American literary criticism became increasingly creative and self- sustaining, persisted until certain individuals, including American Indian writers, began to motivate critics to come to terms with their untidy accomplishments. The focus of existence is quite different for Indians, who persist in remaining as concerned with lived experiences of the "real" world as they are with the world in which imagination moves and has its being.

The task of the critic is to find balance between real and imaginative worlds, yet a tendency in recent American criticism has been to make unnecessary choices between the two, and either to treat literature as a self-sufficient reality of its own or to judge it entirely by extraliterary standards. An example is the way critics have recently attempted to discuss American Indian literature either in terms of creative art or in the context of the authenticity of Indian representation. The discussions that focus on art tend to employ a hybrid romanticism placing the author's authority in his imagination, as expressed through the discourses of art. The discussion focused on authenticity asserts that certain Indian writers, namely mixed-bloods, attempt, but fail, to incorporate authentic American Indian experience, whether or not that is what they are trying to do.

The resulting dichotomy is similar to the attempt to divorce literature from lived experience that made new criticism attractive as a specialized form of modernist practice. In the case of the writers of the American Indian literary renaissance, they are producing not ethnography but imaginative representation, and their use of culturally specific detail supports an artistic rather than representational treatment of subject matter. Substituting unnecessarily problematic interpretations of this situation, where clarity will serve more effectively, creates creative / critical hegemony that discourages contextualization of literary texts. This in turn suppresses a larger range of interactions that then reduces ethnic, class, and gender difference to textual devices.

In reality, American Indian creative writers appropriate a wide range of materials that set up a large number of internal units providing only cursory signals to orient readers, but that is much like lived experience. The texts employ a technique less direct than realism yet more contextually referential than modernism, resulting in the difficulty readers experience in early encounters with texts such as James Welch's *Winter in the Blood* or Louise Erdrich's *Love Medicine*. In the work of both writers, textual puzzles are centered in the texts-within-the-text and signal contextualization as well as ontological difference. This internal textuality is replicated throughout the texts, signaling what Foucault has called an "insurrection of subjugated knowledges" contrasting cultural specificity with modernist devices.[4]

Experience removed from its cultural specificity through any written textual practice makes authenticity elusive, but experience itself is no guarantee of uncontaminated authenticity. While Indianness may be tangled up with literary devices such as modernism, texts that attempt to present it may still preserve much accurate local representation. New-critical hermeticism has provided a convenient means of avoiding contextualization, while other forces have encouraged it in the guise of addressing production and historical context. In addition, literary modernism's suppression of cultural difference effectively marginalized associated realism, defining such realism as a limited literary expression. Despite these influences, the texts of the American Indian literary renaissance resist marginalization while engaging cultural difference, celebrating suppressed and disfranchised knowledges, and presenting a profusion of local information and history.

Effective American Indian critics will avoid polarizing choices such as insistence that literary texts must be defined as either art or ethnography. Instead, they will seek to locate autonomous literary works in a variety of structures as a means of establishing a cultural context for their literary criticism. There should be profound respect for participating in society through the imagination as well as by lived experience, coupled with a deep belief in the formative and educational powers of the study of American Indian literature, both oral and written. A goal of the criticism should be the advancement of two myths from traditional American Indian worldviews: the myth of concern, with its emphasis on social cohesion and what we hold in common, and the myth of individual freedom. The necessary tension between these closed and open attitudes should be resolved slightly in favor of social cohesion; out of this tension between concern and freedom will come glimpses of the experience that poetry urges us to have but that we seldom ever get. This ideal world provides an example of the reconciliation of opposites that is our ultimate ethical goal.

# NOTES

## Introduction

1. Baer, *Warrior: The Life of Leonard Peltier* (Lym Productions, 1991).

2. Hu-DeHart, "The State of Native North America," in *The State of Native America: Genocide, Colonization, and Resistance*, ed. M. Annette Jaimes (1992), ix–x.

3. Fay, *Critical Social Science* (1987), 89.

4. Tierney, *Official Encouragement, Institutional Discouragement: Minorities in Academe—the Native American Experience* (1992), 140.

5. Freire, *Pedagogy of the Oppressed* (1970), 47.

6. Tierney, *Official Encouragement, Institutional Discouragement*, 145.

7. *Shattering the Silences*, prod. Gail Pellett (Gail Pellett Productions, 1997).

8. *Tribal Colleges*, xi.

9. Tierney, *Official Encouragement, Institutional Discouragement*, 117.

10. Deloria, *Custer Died for Your Sins* (1988), 94.

## House Made of Cards
### *The Construction of American Indians*

1. Momaday, "The Man Made of Words," in *Indian Voices: The First Convocation of American Indian Scholars* (1970), 55.

2. Owens, *Other Destinies: Understanding the American Indian Novel* (1992), 4.

3. Kenneth Lincoln, *Indi'n Humor: Bicultural Play in Native America* (1993), 4.

4. Trilling, *The Opposing Self* (1978), 33. In *The Liberal Imagination: Essays on Literature and Society*, Trilling also says that it is the very essence of intelligence to recognize irresolvable complexity (281).

5. Timothy Egan, "Nez Perce Anticipate a Homecoming," *Eugene (Oreg.) Register-Guard* (July 22, 1996): 1A, 5A.

6. Kenneth Lincoln, *Native American Renaissance* (1983), 10.

7. Berkhofer, *The White Man's Indian: Images of the American Indian from Columbus to the Present* (1979). The notes section of Berkhofer's book summarizes a substantial body of earlier scholarship. In addition, Richard Drinnon's *Facing West: The Metaphysics of Indian Hating and Empire Building* and James Clifford's *The Predicament of Culture* are perceptive views. Drinnon's text is divided into "Maypoles and Pequots," "Founding Fathers and Merciless Savages," "Philanthropists and Indian-Haters," "Civilizers and Conquerors," and "Children of Light," which brings his discussion up through the Vietnam era. Clifford's text is divided into "Discourses," "Displacements," "Collections," and "Histories," an enlightening look at the Mashpee trial, wherein the Mashpee sued to establish their Indian identity in court.

8. Lincoln, *Native American Renaissance*, 10.

9. Wiget, *Native American Literature* (1985), 121; Ruoff, *American Indian Literatures* (1990).

10. Lincoln, *Native American Renaissance*, ix.

11. Warrior, *Tribal Secrets* (1995), xvi.

12. Lincoln, *Native American Renaissance*, 11.

13. Owens, *Other Destinies*, 5.

14. Lincoln, *Indi'n Humor*, 10.

15. Forbes, "Colonialism," *Wicazo Sa Review* 3 (1987): 19; Krupat, *The Voice in the Margin: Native American Literature and the Canon* (1989), 207.

16. Geiogamah, *Foghorn, Native American Literature: A Brief Introduction and Anthology*, ed. Gerald Vizenor (1995), 349.

17. Clifton, *Being and Becoming Indian: Biographical Studies of North American Frontiers* (1989), 22.

18. Berkhofer, *The White Man's Indian*, xvi.

19. Proposed Rules, *Federal Register* 56, no. 181 (September 18, 1991).

20. In *"Race," Writing, and Difference*, ed. Henry Louis Gates Jr. (1986), 384, 405.

21. Clifton, *Being and Becoming Indian*, 17.

22. Ibid., 9.

23. Harjo, "The Story of All Our Survival," in *Survival This Way*, ed. Joseph Bruchac (1987), 5, 6.

24. Clifford, *The Predicament of Culture: Twentieth-Century Ethnography, Literature, and Art* (1988), 8.

25. McMurtry, *Lonesome Dove* (1985), 935.

26. Clearman-Blew, letter to the author, May 15, 1992.

## American Indians, Authenticity, and the Future

1. Anonymous remarks proffered as "Reader's Comments" to a refereed academic journal that shall also remain nameless.

2. Arnold Krupat, "Scholarship and Native American Studies: A Response to Daniel Littlefield, Jr.," *American Studies* 34:2 (1993): 81–100.

3. Deloria, *Custer Died for Your Sins* (1988), 215.

4. Littlefield, "American Indians," *American Studies* 33:2 (1992): 95–112. I have selected only portions from this article and strongly suggest a full reading.

5. Elizabeth Cook-Lynn, "American Indian Intellectualism and the New Indian Story," *American Indian Quarterly* 20:1 (winter 1996): 57–76.

6. Krupat, *The Turn to the Native*, 42.

7. Ibid., 43.

8. Vizenor, *The Heirs of Columbus* (1991), 16.

9. Krupat, *The Turn to the Native*, 83.

10. Ibid., 80, 81.

11. Trilling, *Beyond Culture: Essays on Literature and Learning* (1978), 178; Trilling, *The Last Decade: Essays and Reviews, 1965–1975*, ed. Diana Trilling (1977), 146–47.

12. Trilling, *The Last Decade*, 123.

13. Diana Trilling, ed., *Speaking of Literature and Society*, Uniform Edition (1980), 120–21.

14. Boyarin, *Storm from Paradise: The Politics of Jewish Memory*, 10.

15. Stannard, *American Holocaust* (1992), x.

16. Dobyns, *Their Number Become Thinned: Native American Population Dynamics in Eastern North America* (1983), 42, 342–43.

17. Stannard, *American Holocaust*, xi.

18. From the testimony of Maj. Scott J. Anthony, First Colorado Cavalry, before United States Congress, House of Representatives: "Massacre of Cheyenne Indians," in *Report on the Conduct of the War*, 38th Cong., 2nd Sess., 1865, 27.

19. Linton, "The 'Person' in Postmodern Fiction," *SAIL* 5:3 (fall 1993): 3–11.

20. Goldberg, *Multiculturalism: A Critical Reader* (1994), 26.

21. Moyes, "Into the Fray: Literary Studies at the Juncture of Feminist/Fiction Theory," in *Canada: Theoretical Discourse/Discours théoriques*, ed. Terry Goldie, Carmen Lambert, and Rowland Lorimer (1994), 309.

22. Emberley, *Thresholds of Difference* (1993), 5.

23. Goldberg, *Multiculturalism*, 26.

24. Williamson, *Sounding Differences* (1993), 290.

25. Silko, *Ceremony* (1977), 2.

## Vine Deloria Jr.
### Reconstructing the Logic of Belief

1. Warrior, *Tribal Secrets* (1994), 61–62.

2. Magnus, "Postmodern Pragmatism: Nietzsche, Heidegger, Derrida, and Rorty," in *Pragmatism: From Progressivism to Postmodernism*, ed. Robert Hollinger and David Depew (1995), 278.

3. Gunn, "Pragmatism, Democracy, and the Imagination," in ibid., 308.

4. Ibid., 309.

5. Deloria, *God Is Red* (1994), 178.

6. A central consideration of postapocalypse theory is that American Indians have already lived through an "end of the world" and are thus more free to work toward unification of the past and future with the present.

7. Deloria, *God Is Red*, 85.

8. John Dewey, "Thought and Its Subject-Matter," in *Studies in Logical Theory*, University of Chicago Decennial Publications, 2nd ser., vol. 11 (1903), 8.

9. Deloria, *God Is Red*, 215.

10. Deloria, *Custer Died for Your Sins* (1988), 84.

11. Deloria, *God Is Red*, 65, 73.

12. Ibid., 66.

13. Deloria, *Custer Died for Your Sins*, 228.

14. Scott L. Pratt, unpublished lecture, University of Oregon, 1977.

## Constituting and Preserving Self through Writing

1. Gusdorf, "Conditions and Limits of Autobiography," in *Autobiography: Essays Theoretical and Critical*, ed. James Olney (1988), 45.

2. Bush, "The Personal Statement of Barney Bush," in *I Tell You Now: Autobiographical Essays by Native American Writers*, ed. Brian Swann and Arnold Krupat (1987), 221.

3. Simpson, "Soldier's Heart," *Hudson Review* (winter 1997): 550.

4. Silko, "Language and Literature from a Pueblo Indian Perspective," in *Literature: Opening Up the Canon*, ed. Fiedler and Baker, (1981), 60.

5. Warrior, *Tribal Secrets: Vine Deloria, Jr., John Joseph Mathews, and the Recovery of American Indian Intellectual Traditions* (1993), 183.

6. Gilman, "What Should Scholarly Publication in the Humanities Be?" *MLA Newsletter* (fall 1995): 4.

7. Arnold Krupat, in "Native American Autobiography and the Synecdochic Self," discusses the metaphorical conception of self as well as metonymy and synecdoche as relations of part-to-part and part-to-whole. Where the self as the object of conscious and developed concern is de-emphasized, concern about the unreliable narrator is lessened as well.

## Louise Erdrich
### *Protecting and Celebrating Culture*

1. Allen, *The Sacred Hoop: Recovering the Feminine in American Indian Traditions* (1986), 262, 172.

2. Warrior, *Tribal Secrets: Vine Deloria, Jr., John Joseph Mathews, and the Recovery of American Indian Intellectual Traditions* (1993), 181.

3. Janet McCloud, "Open Letter," 329.

4. Erdrich, "Where I Ought to Be: A Writer's Sense of Place," *New York Times Book Review* (July 28, 1985).

5. Allen, *Sacred Hoop*, 79.

6. Klein, "The Political-Economy of Gender: A Nineteenth-Century Plains Indian Case Study," in *The Hidden Half: Studies of Plains Indian Women*, ed. Patricia Albers and Beatrice Medicine (1983), 150–51.

7. Ibid., 220.

8. Rabinow, "Representations Are Social Facts: Modernity and Post-Modernity in Anthropology," in *Writing Culture: The Poetics and Politics of Ethnography*, ed. James Clifford and George Marcus (1986).

9. Silko, "Pueblo Indian Perspective," in *English Literature: Selected Papers from the English Institute, 1979*, ed. Leslie Fiedler and Houston Baker (1981), 56–57.

10. Geertz, "Deep Play: Notes on the Balinese Cockfight," in *The Interpretation of Cultures: Selected Essays by Clifford Geertz* (1973), 453.

11. A. LaVonne Brown Ruoff, *American Indian Literatures: An Introduction, Bibliographic Review, and Selected Bibliography* (1990), 85.

12. Jaimes, "American Indian Studies: Toward an Indigenous Model," *American Indian Culture and Research Journal* 11:3 (1987): 1–16. Jaimes's work foregrounds that of Cornel West, who, in his widely publicized book *Race Matters*, exhorts academics to remain connected to their communities of origin after achieving a place in the academy.

13. Marvin Magalener, "Of Cars, Time, and the River," in *American Women Writing Fiction: Memory, Identity, Family Space*, ed. Mickey Pearlman (1989), 96. I feel strongly that the suggestion of prostitution is not supported by the book, seems moralistic and perhaps racist, and is simply not appropriate.

14. McKenzie, "Lipsha's Good Road Home," *American Indian Culture and Research Journal* 10:3 (1986): 53–63; Erdrich, *Love Medicine* (1984), 3. Subsequent references will be cited parenthetically.

15. Schneider, *North Dakota Indians* (1986), 91.

16. Robert P. Wilkins and Winona H. Wilkins, *North Dakota: A History* (1977), 31.

17. Maristuen-Rodakowski, "The Turtle Mountain Reservation in North Dakota: Its History as Depicted in Louise Erdrich's *Love Medicine* and *Beet Queen*," *American Indian Culture and Research Journal* 12:3 (1988): 40.

18. Welch, *Winter in the Blood* (1974), 5.

19. Hartmann, "The Significance of the Pipe" (master's thesis, Montana State University, 1955), 8.

20. Rainwater, "Reading between Worlds," *American Literature* 62 (September 1990): 405–6.

21. Devereaux, *Mohave Ethnopsychiatry* (1969), 130.

22. Unrau, *Mixed-Bloods and Tribal Dissolution* (1989), 135.

23. Erdrich, *Tracks* (1988), 4. Subsequent references will be cited parenthetically.

24. Welch, *Winter in the Blood*, 40.

25. Rainwater, "Reading between Worlds," 409.

26. Castillo, "Postmodernism, Native American Literature and the Real: The Silko-Erdrich Controversy," *Massachusetts Review* 32:2 (1991): 288.

27. Ibid., 292–93.

28. Ibid., 294.

29. Warrior, *Tribal Secrets*, 85.

## James Welch's *Indian Lawyer*

1. Owens, *Other Destinies: Understanding the American Indian Novel* (1992), 92.

2. Beidler, "A Symposium Issue on James Welch's *Winter in the Blood*," *American Indian Quarterly* 4:1 (1978): 95.

3. For other kinds of discussions associated with *Winter in the Blood*, see Elaine Jahner, "Quick Paces and a Space of Mind," *Denver Quarterly* 14:4 (1980): 34–47; and William Thackeray, "Crying for Pity in *Winter in the Blood*," *MELUS* 7:1 (spring 1980): 61–78.

4. Bevis, "Dialogue with James Welch," *Northwest Review* 20:2–3 (1982): 168, 169.

5. Krupat, "Native American Autobiography," *American Autobiography: Retrospect and Prospect* (1991), 178.

6. See Bevis, "Dialogue with James Welch," 166–67.

7. Welch, *Winter in the Blood* (1974), 1. Subsequent references will be cited parenthetically.

8. Welch, *The Death of Jim Loney* (1979), 3, 127, 167.

9. Welch, *Fools Crow* (1986), 81. Subsequent references will be cited parenthetically.

10. For the historical context of such stories, see Roy Harvey Pearce, *The Savages of America: A Study of the Indian and the Idea of Civilization* (Baltimore: Johns Hopkins, 1965); Richard Slotkin, *Regeneration through Violence: The Mythology of the American Frontier, 1600–1860* (Middletown, Conn.: Wesleyan University Press, 1973); and Richard Drinnon, *Facing West: The*

*Metaphysics of Indian-Hating and Empire-Building* (New York: New American Library, 1980).

11. Owens, *Other Destinies*, 3.

12. Welch, *The Indian Lawyer* (1990), 249. Subsequent references will be cited parenthetically. Riesman, *The Lonely Crowd* (1950). Riesman's concepts have been around long enough to be considered almost common knowledge. They are still valid, however, and I include the citation for those interested in more-thorough discussion.

13. McFee, "The 150% Man," *American Anthropologist* 70:6 (1968): 1096–1103; McFee's *Modern Blackfeet* (1972) was reprinted in 1992 and continues to accurately reflect groupings of which I am aware at Fort Belknap, where I am from, as well as at the Blackfeet reservation.

14. Velie, "American Indian Literature in the Nineties: The Emergence of the Middle-Class Protagonist," *World Literature Today* 66:2 (1992): 265.

15. Bevis, "Dialogue with James Welch," 169, 172.

16. Velie, "American Indian Literature in the Nineties," 264.

17. Gish, "New Warrior, New West," *American Indian Quarterly* 15:3 (1991): 372.

18. Smith, "Shadow of a Nation," *Sports Illustrated* (February 18, 1991): 64, 65.

19. Kroeber, *Retelling/Rereading: The Fate of Storytelling in Modern Times* (1990), 78, 79.

20. Ibid., 62.

21. Posner, *Law and Literature: A Misunderstood Relation* (1988), 284, 285–86.

22. Ibid., 161–62.

23. Jameson, *The Prison-House of Language* (1972), 119.

24. Clifford, *The Predicament of Culture: Twentieth-Century Ethnography, Literature, and Art* (1988), 10.

## Pragmatism and American Indian Thought

1. Warrior, *Tribal Secrets* (1994), 61–62.

2. Dewey, "Thought and Its Subject-Matter," in *Studies in Logical Theory*, University of Chicago Decennial Publications, 2nd ser., vol 11 (1903), 8.

3. Neihardt, *Black Elk Speaks* (1972), 233.

4. Lincoln, *Native American Renaissance* (1983), 89.

5. Pratt, "The Influence of the Iroquois on Early American Philosophy" (1996), 28.

6. Gourevitch, "Letter from Rwanda: After the Genocide," *New Yorker* (December 18, 1995): 87.

7. Gunn, "Pragmatism, Democracy, and the Imagination: Rethinking the Deweyan Legacy," in *Pragmatism: From Progressivism to Postmodernism*, ed. Robert Hollinger and David Depew (1995), 305. Subsequent references will be cited parenthetically.

8. West, "Theory, Pragmatisms, and Politics," in ibid., 323.

9. Remnick, "The War for the Kremlin," *New Yorker* (July 22, 1996): 43.

10. MacKenzie, "Pragmatism, Rhetoric, and History," *Poetics Today* 16:2 (summer 1995): 284. Subsequent references will be cited parenthetically. Stevens, *Opus Posthumous*, ed. Milton J. Bates (1988).

11. Rorty, *Contingency, Irony and Solidarity* (1989), 7.

12. A. L. Kroeber, "Gros Ventre Myths and Tales," in *Anthropological Papers of the American Museum of Natural History*, ed. Clark Wissler (1908), 59–61; Flannery, *The Gros Ventres of Montana* (1953).

13. Converse, *Myths and Legends of the New York State Iroquois*, ed. Arthur C. Parker (1908), 32–34.

14. Parker, "The Code of Handsome Lake," in *Parker on the Iroquois*, ed. William N. Fenton (1968), 17.

15. Noyes, *In the Land of Chinook: The Story of Blaine County* (1917), 9–10.

16. Schubnell, *N. Scott Momaday: The Cultural and Literary Background* (1985), 97.

17. Owens, *Other Destinies: Understanding the American Indian Novel* (1992), 105.

18. Silko, *Ceremony* (1977), 120. Subsequent references will be cited parenthetically.

19. Silko, "Here's an Odd Artifact for the Fairy-Tale Shelf," review of *The Beet Queen*, by Louise Erdrich, *Studies in American Indian Literature* 10 (1986): 179.

20. Castillo, "Postmodernism, Native American Literature and the Real: The Silko-Erdrich Controversy," *Massachusetts Review* 32:2 (1991): 285. Subsequent references will be cited parenthetically.

21. Forbes, "Colonialism and Native American Literature: Analysis," *Wicazo Sa Review* 3 (1987): 17–23.

22. Warrior, *Tribal Secrets*, 84.

## Conclusion

1. Boyarin, *Storm from Paradise: The Politics of Jewish Memory* (1992), 90. Subsequent references will be cited parenthetically.

2. Stannard, *American Holocaust* (1992), x.

3. Deloria, *God Is Red* (1994), 1–2.

4. Michel Foucault, *Power/Knowledge: Selected Interviews and Other Writings, 1972–1977*, ed. Colin Gordon (1980), 81.

# BIBLIOGRAPHY

ALLEN, PAULA GUNN. *The Sacred Hoop: Recovering the Feminine in American Indian Traditions*. Boston: Beacon Press, 1986.

BAKER, HOUSTON. "Caliban's Triple Play." In *"Race," Writing, and Difference*, ed. Henry Louis Gates Jr. Chicago: University of Chicago Press, 1986.

BEIDLER, PETER G. "A Symposium Issue on James Welch's *Winter in the Blood*." *American Indian Quarterly* 4:1 (1978): 95.

BERKHOFER, ROBERT F., JR. *The White Man's Indian: Images of the American Indian from Columbus to the Present*. New York: Vintage Books, 1979.

BEVIS, WILLIAM W. "Dialogue with James Welch." *Northwest Review* 20: 2–3 (1982): 168.

BOYARIN, JONATHAN. *Storm from Paradise: The Politics of Jewish Memory*. Minneapolis: University of Minnesota Press, 1992.

BUSH, BARNEY. "The Personal Statement of Barney Bush." In *I Tell You Now: Autobiographical Essays by Native American Writers*, ed. Brian Swann and Arnold Krupat. Lincoln: University of Nebraska Press, 1987.

CASTILLO, SUSAN PEREZ. "Postmodernism, Native American Literature and the Real: The Silko-Erdrich Controversy." *Massachusetts Review* 32:2 (1991): 288.

CLIFFORD, JAMES. *The Predicament of Culture: Twentieth-Century Ethnography, Literature, and Art.* Cambridge: Harvard University Press, 1988.

CLIFTON, JAMES. *Being and Becoming Indian: Biographical Studies of North American Frontiers.* Chicago: Dorsey Press, 1989.

CONVERSE, HARRIET MAXWELL. *Myths and Legends of the New York State Iroquois.* Ed. Arthur C. Parker. New York State Museum and Sciences Service Bulletin 125, 1908.

COOK-LYNN, ELIZABETH. "American Indian Intellectualism and the New Indian Story." *American Indian Quarterly* 20:1 (winter 1996): 57–76.

DELORIA, VINE, JR. *Custer Died for Your Sins.* New York: Macmillan, 1969. Reprint, Norman: University of Oklahoma Press, 1988.

——. *God Is Red.* New York: Grosset and Dunlap, 1973. Rev. ed., Golden, Colo.: Fulcrum Publishing, 1994.

DEVEREAUX, GEORGES. *Mohave Ethnopsychiatry.* Washington: Smithsonian Institution Press, 1969.

DEWEY, JOHN. "Thought and Its Subject-Matter." *Studies in Logical Theory.* University of Chicago Decennial Publications. 2nd series, vol. 11. Chicago: University of Chicago Press, 1903.

DOBYNS, HENRY F. *Their Number Became Thinned: Native American Population Dynamics in Eastern North America.* Knoxville: University of Tennessee Press, 1983.

EGAN, TIMOTHY. "Nez Perce Anticipate a Homecoming." *Eugene (Oreg.) Register-Guard* (July 22, 1996): 1A, 5A.

EMBERLEY, JULIA V. *Thresholds of Difference: Feminist Critique, Native Women's Writings, Postcolonial Theory.* Toronto: University of Toronto Press, 1993.

ERDRICH, LOUISE. *Love Medicine.* New York: Holt, 1984. New, exp. ed., New York: Harper Perennial, 1993.

——. *Tracks.* New York: Harper and Row, 1988.

——. "Where I Ought to Be: A Writer's Sense of Place." *New York Times Book Review* (July 28, 1985).

FAY, BRIAN. *Critical Social Science.* Ithaca: Cornell University Press, 1987.

FLANNERY, REGINA. *The Gros Ventres of Montana.* Washington, D.C.: Catholic University of America Press, 1953.

FORBES, JACK. "Colonialism and Native American Literature: Analysis." *Wicazo Sa Review* 3 (1987): 17–23.

FOUCAULT, MICHEL. *Power/Knowledge: Selected Interviews and Other Writings, 1972–1977.* Ed. Colin Gordon. New York: Pantheon, 1980.

FREIRE, PAOLO. *Pedagogy of the Oppressed*. New York: Seabury Press, 1970.

GATES, HENRY LOUIS, JR., ed. *"Race," Writing, and Difference*. Chicago: University of Chicago Press, 1986.

GEERTZ, CLIFFORD. "Deep Play: Notes on the Balinese Cockfight." In *The Interpretation of Cultures: Selected Essays by Clifford Geertz*. New York: Basic Books, 1973.

GEIOGAMAH, HANAY. *Foghorn, Native American Literature: A Brief Introduction and Anthology*. Ed. Gerald Vizenor. Berkeley and Los Angeles: HarperCollins College Publishers, 1995.

GIBSON, WILLIAM. *Neuromancer*. New York: Ace Books, 1984.

GILMAN, SANDER. "What Should Scholarly Publication in the Humanities Be?" *MLA Newsletter* (fall 1995): 4.

GISH, ROBERT F. "New Warrior, New West: History and Advocacy in James Welch's *The Indian Lawyer*." *American Indian Quarterly* 15:3 (1991): 372.

GOLDBERG, DAVID THEO. *Multiculturalism: A Critical Reader*. Oxford: Blackwell, 1994.

GOUREVITCH, PHILIP. "Letter from Rwanda: After the Genocide." *New Yorker* (December 18, 1995): 87.

GUNN, GILES. "Pragmatism, Democracy, and the Imagination." In *Pragmatism: From Progressivism to Postmodernism*, ed. Robert Hollinger and David Depew. Westport, Conn.: Praeger, 1995.

GUSDORF, GEORGES. "Conditions and Limits of Autobiography." In *Autobiography: Essays Theoretical and Critical*, ed. James Olney. Princeton: Princeton University Press, 1988.

HARJO, JOY. "The Story of All Our Survival." In *Survival This Way*, ed. Joseph Bruchac. Tucson: University of Arizona Press, 1987.

HARTMANN, SISTER M. CLARE. "The Significance of the Pipe to the Gros Ventres of Montana." Master's thesis, Montana State University, 1955.

HU-DEHART, EVELYN. "The State of Native North America." In *The State of Native America: Genocide, Colonization, and Resistance*, ed. M. Annette Jaimes. Boston: South End Press, 1992.

JAIMES, ANNETTE. "American Indian Studies: Toward an Indigenous Model." *American Indian Culture and Research Journal* 11:3 (1987): 1–16.

JAMESON, FREDRIC. *The Prison-House of Language*. Princeton: Princeton University Press, 1972.

KLEIN, ALAN M. "The Political-Economy of Gender: A Nineteenth-Century

Plains Indian Case Study." In *The Hidden Half: Studies of Plains Indian Women*, ed. Patricia Albers and Beatrice Medicine. New York: University Press of America, 1983.

KROEBER, A. L. "Gros Ventre Myths and Tales." In *Anthropological Papers of the American Museum of Natural History*, ed. Clark Wissler. New York: American Museum of Natural History Trustees, 1908.

KROEBER, KARL. *Retelling/Rereading: The Fate of Storytelling in Modern Times*. New Brunswick: Rutgers University Press, 1990.

KRUPAT, ARNOLD. "Scholarship and Native American Studies: A Response to Daniel Littlefield, Jr." *American Studies* 34:2 (1993): 81–100.

———. *The Voice in the Margin: Native American Literature and the Canon*. Berkeley and Los Angeles: University of California Press, 1989.

LINCOLN, KENNETH. *Indi'n Humor*. New York: Oxford University Press, 1993.

———. *Native American Renaissance*. Berkeley and Los Angeles: University of California Press, 1983.

LINTON, PATRICIA. "The 'Person' in Postmodern Fiction: Gibson, LeGuin, and Vizenor." *SAIL* 5:3 (fall 1993): 3–11.

LITTLEFIELD, DANIEL F., JR. "American Indians, American Scholars, and the American Literary Canon." *American Studies* 33:2 (1992): 95–112.

MACKENZIE, IAN. "Pragmatism, Rhetoric, and History." *Poetics Today* 16:2 (summer 1995): 284.

MAGALENER, MARVIN. "Of Cars, Time, and the River." In *American Women Writing Fiction: Memory, Identity, Family Space*, ed. Mickey Pearlman. Lexington: University Press of Kentucky, 1989.

MAGNUS, BERND. "Postmodern Pragmatism: Nietzsche, Heidegger, Derrida, and Rorty." In *Pragmatism: From Progressivism to Postmodernism*, ed. Robert Hollinger and David Depew. Westport, Conn.: Praeger, 1995.

MARISTUEN-RODAKOWSKI, JULIE. "The Turtle Mountain Reservation in North Dakota: Its History as Depicted in Louise Erdrich's *Love Medicine* and *Beet Queen*." *American Indian Culture and Research Journal* 12:3 (1988): 40.

MCCLOUD, JANET. "Open Letter." In *The State of Native America: Genocide, Colonization, and Resistance*, ed. M. Annette Jaimes. Boston: South End Press, 1992.

MCFEE, MALCOLM. *Modern Blackfeet: Montanans on a Reservation*. Prospect Heights, Ill.: Waveland Press, 1972.

MCKENZIE, JAMES. "Lipsha's Good Road Home." *American Indian Culture and Research Journal* 10:3 (1986): 53–63.

MCMURTRY, LARRY. *Lonesome Dove*. New York: Simon and Schuster, 1985.

MOMADAY, N. SCOTT. "The Man Made of Words." In *Indian Voices: The First Convocation of American Indian Scholars*. San Francisco: Indian Historian Press, 1970.

MOYES, LIANNE. "Into the Fray: Literary Studies at the Juncture of Feminist/Fiction Theory." In *Canada: Theoretical Discourse/Discours théoriques*, ed. Terry Goldie, Carmen Lambert, and Rowland Lorimer. Montreal: Association for Canadian Studies, 1994.

NEIHARDT, JOHN. *Black Elk Speaks*. New York: Simon and Schuster, 1972.

NOYES, A. J. *In the Land of Chinook: The Story of Blaine County*. Helena: State Publishing, 1917.

OWENS, LOUIS. *Other Destinies: Understanding the American Indian Novel*. Norman: University of Oklahoma Press, 1992.

PARKER, ARTHUR C. "The Code of Handsome Lake." In *Parker on the Iroquois*, ed. William N. Fenton. Syracuse: Syracuse University Press, 1968.

POSNER, RICHARD A. *Law and Literature: A Misunderstood Relation*. Cambridge: Harvard University Press, 1988.

RABINOW, PAUL. "Representations Are Social Facts: Modernity and Post-Modernity in Anthropology." In *Writing Culture: The Poetics and Politics of Ethnography*, ed. James Clifford and George Marcus. Berkeley and Los Angeles: University of California Press, 1986.

RAINWATER, CATHERINE. "Reading between Worlds: Narrativity in the Fiction of Louise Erdrich." *American Literature* 62 (September 1990): 405–6.

REMNICK, DAVID. "The War for the Kremlin." *New Yorker* (July 22, 1996): 43.

RIESMAN, DAVID. *The Lonely Crowd*. New Haven: Yale University Press, 1950.

RORTY, RICHARD. *Contingency, Irony, and Solidarity*. Cambridge: Cambridge University Press, 1989.

RUOFF, A. LAVONNE BROWN. *American Indian Literatures*. New York: Modern Language Association of America, 1990.

SCHEICK, WILLIAM J. *The Half-Blood*. Lexington: University Press of Kentucky, 1979.

SCHNEIDER, MARY JANE. *North Dakota Indians*. Dubuque: Kendall/Hunt Publishing, 1986.

SCHUBNELL, MATTHIAS. *N. Scott Momaday: The Cultural and Literary Background.* Norman: University of Oklahoma Press, 1985.

SHATTERING THE SILENCES. Produced by Gail Pellett. Gail Pellett Productions, 1997.

SILKO, LESLIE MARMON. *Ceremony.* New York: Penguin, 1977.

———. "Here's an Odd Artifact for the Fairy-Tale Shelf." Review of *The Beet Queen*, by Louise Erdrich. *Studies in American Indian Literature* 10 (1986): 179.

———. "Language and Literature from a Pueblo Indian Perspective." *Literature: Opening Up the Canon.* Baltimore: Johns Hopkins University Press, 1981.

SIMPSON, LOUIS. "Soldier's Heart." *Hudson Review* (winter 1997): 550.

SMITH, GARY. "Shadow of a Nation." *Sports Illustrated* (February 18, 1991): 64.

STANNARD, DAVID. *American Holocaust.* New York: Oxford University Press, 1992.

STEVENS, WALLACE. *Opus Posthumous.* Ed. Milton J. Bates. New York: Vintage, 1988.

TIERNEY, WILLIAM G. *Official Encouragement, Institutional Discouragement: Minorities in Academe—The Native American Experience.* Norwood, N.J.: Ablex Publishing, 1992.

TRILLING, LIONEL. *Beyond Culture: Essays on Literature and Learning.* New York: Harcourt Brace Jovanovich, 1978.

———. *The Opposing Self: Nine Essays in Criticism.* New York: Harcourt Brace Jovanovich, 1978.

UNRAU, WILLIAM. *Mixed-Bloods and Tribal Dissolution: Charles Curtis and the Quest for Indian Identity.* Lawrence: University Press of Kansas, 1989.

VELIE, ALAN R. "American Indian Literature in the Nineties: The Emergence of the Middle-Class Protagonist." *World Literature Today* 6:2 (1992): 265.

VIZENOR, GERALD. *The Heirs of Columbus.* Hanover: Wesleyan University Press, 1991.

WARRIOR: THE LIFE OF LEONARD PELTIER. Produced by Suzie Baer. Lym Productions, 1991.

WARRIOR, ROBERT ALLEN. *Tribal Secrets: Recovering American Indian Intellectual Traditions.* Minneapolis: University of Minnesota Press, 1995.

———. *Tribal Secrets: Vine Deloria, Jr., John Joseph Mathews, and the Recov-*

*ery of American Indian Intellectual Traditions.* Ann Arbor: UMI Dissertation Services, 1994.

WELCH, JAMES. *Fools Crow.* New York: Viking Penguin, 1986.

———. *The Indian Lawyer.* New York: Norton, 1990.

———. *Winter in the Blood.* New York: Harper and Row, 1974.

WEST, CORNEL. "Theory, Pragmatisms, and Politics." In *Pragmatism: From Progressivism to Postmodernism,* ed. Robert Hollinger and David Depew. Westport, Conn.: Praeger, 1995.

WIGET, ANDREW. *Native American Literature.* Boston: Twayne, 1985.

WILKINS, ROBERT P., and WINONA H. WILKINS. *North Dakota: A History.* New York: Norton, 1977.

WILLIAMSON, JANICE. *Sounding Differences: Conversations with Seventeen Canadian Women Writers.* Toronto: University of Toronto Press, 1993.

# INDEX

Absolute principles, 28
acculturation, 24, 40
*All but the Waltz* (Clearman-Blew),
    38
allegory, 22, 48
Allen, Paula Gunn, 81–82, 84
American history, 4
American holocaust, 42, 49
American Indian Movement, 46
*American Indian Quarterly*, 105
American Indians: as topic of inter-
    est in higher education, 5; pri-
    mary values of, 6; and academic
    achievement, 13; as perceived in
    the classroom, 14; resistance to as-
    similation, 23; literary criticism
    by, 56; women writers, 80, 81; and
    basketball, 116–17
*American Indians, American Schol-*
*ars, and the American Literary*
*Canon* (Littlefield), 43
Amish, 64
*Ancient Child, The* (Momaday),
    44
anthropology, 86
antihero in American Indian writ-
    ing, 24
Appiah, Kwame Anthony, 44
Armstrong, Jeannette, 54–55
assimilation, 23
authenticity debate: and intellec-
    tual sovereignty, 27; and identity,
    27, 45; and redescription, 38; and
    issues within, 41; and Vine Delo-
    ria Jr., 42; and Arnold Krupat, 43;
    and cultural ownership, 43; and
    negative capability, 48, 147; and
    autobiography, 70

autobiography, 3, 26, 70, 71–72, 76, 77, 106–7

Baker, Houston, 32–33
Baker Massacre, 109, 124
*Balsamroot* (Clearman-Blew), 38
basketball, 116–17
*Beet Queen, The* (Erdrich), 101, 142
Beidler, Peter G., 105
Benjamin, Walter, 153
Berkhofer, Robert F., Jr., 24, 31, 158 n. 7
Bevis, William, 106
bicultural, 4
*Black Elk Speaks*, 130
Black Hawk, 26
Black Hills, S.D., 8
blood quantum, 31, 34, 36
Blue Duck, 31, 37
Boyarin, Jonathan, 49, 145, 146, 147, 151, 153
Boyer, Paul, 15
"Breeds," 39
*brûle*, 30, 90
Bureau of Indian Affairs (BIA), 15, 32, 42
Burlington-Northern, 8
Bush, Barney, 70
Butler, Octavia, 51

Campbell, Maria, 37, 55
capitalism, 25
Castillo, Susan Perez, 101, 142
*Catch Colt* (Larson), 72–73
Catholicism, 90, 91
*Ceremony* (Silko), 44, 140–41
Chambeaux, Louis, 78
Chevron, 8

Chivington, John, 50
Christianity, 60, 148
circle, American Indian concept of, 56
circular thinking, contrasted to linear thinking, 59
class size and academic achievement, 12–13
Clearman-Blew, Mary, 38
Clifford, James: and identity, 26, 35; and racial classification, 30; *The Predicament of Culture*, 127; and "serious fictions," 127
*Cogewea* (Mourning Dove), 37
Colden, Cadwallader, 131
Collier, John, 44
colonization, 7, 9, 24, 49
color and racial classification, 30
Conoco, 8
Coppola, Francis, 58
Culleton, Beatrice, 55
cultural ownership and the authenticity debate, 43
cultural superiority, 10, 15
Curtis, Charles, 93
Custer, George Armstrong, 64
*Custer Died for Your Sins* (Deloria), 42, 43, 64

Dawes Severalty Act, 33, 78, 89
*Dead Voices* (Vizenor), 45
death, 6, 7, 60, 62
*Death of Jim Loney, The* (Welch): and American Indian identity, 37; as second-stage novel, 44; and interracial relationships, 109–10
Decker Coal, 8

Deloria, Vine, Jr.: and criticism of higher education, 17; compared to Northrop Frye, 19; seminar on, 40; and authenticity debate, 42; *Custer Died for Your Sins*, 42, 43, 64; and pragmatism, 59, 129; on attitudes to death, 60, 62; *God Is Red*, 60, 63, 65; and community and place, 66; and rhetorical strategies, 68; and comparison of American Indians and Jews, 148

Devereaux, George, 92

Dewey, John, 129

double bind, 13, 14, 43

dream culture, 7

Durham, Jimmie, 35, 72, 82

Eakin, John Paul, 77

Eastman, Charles, 26

education, 3, 4, 5, 6, 10, 12, 15, 16

Ellison, Bruce, 8

Emberley, Julia, 55

Erdrich, Louise: and ethnography, 25; *Love Medicine*, 84; and storytelling, 84; and mixed-blood, 87; *Tracks*, 89; *The Beet Queen*, 101; and pragmatism, 141

essentialism, 27, 43, 81

ethnic professors, 13–14

Euramerican principles and identity, 31

exclusion: and strategies of writing and representation, 31; as strategy to reduce American Indian numbers, 32; methods of, 34

exclusivist territoriality, 17

Exxon, 8

Family: and violence, 58, 72; and matriarchy, 78

Fay, Brian, 10

FBI, 8

*Federal Register*, 32

feminism and American Indian women, 7, 80, 81

Flannery, Regina, 137

*Foghorn* (Geiogamah), 29

*Fools Crow* (Welch), 108

Forbes, Jack, 28, 36

Fort Belknap Reservation, 5, 39, 124

Fort Laramie Treaty of 1868, 8

Foucault, Michel, 154

Freire, Paolo, 12

Frye, Northrop, 19

Gates, Henry Louis, Jr., 33

Geiogamah, Hanay, 29

gender, 81

General Allotment/Dawes Act of 1887, 33, 78, 89

Generation X, 6

genocide, 60, 61, 147–49; of American Indians, 5, 42, 49; as an ongoing policy, 17; rationalization and denial of, 21; consequences of, 40; acknowledgment of, 48; and scholarship, 58; and postapocalypse theory, 144

Gibson, William, 51, 52

Gilman, Sander, 76

Gish, Robert F., 113

*Godfather, The* (movie), 58

*God Is Red* (Deloria), 60, 63, 65

Goldberg, David, 53

Gourevitch, Philip, 58, 132–33

*Griever* (Vizenor), 37

Gros Ventre Indians, 5, 29, 137
Gunn, Giles, 61, 133–34
Gunnars, Kristjana, 54
Gusdorf, George, 70

*Half-Blood, The* (Scheick), 37
half-breed, 30, 90
*Halfbreed* (Campbell), 37, 55
Harjo, Joy, 35
*Heirs of Columbus, The* (Vizenor), 45
heterogeneity: and tokenism, 13; compared to multiculturalism, 17
holocaust, 42, 49, 148
Homestead Acts, 8
*House Made of Dawn* (Momaday), 44, 140
Hu-DeHart, Evelyn, 9
humor and naming, 27
*Hunger of Memory* (Rodriguez), 77
Hutcheon, Linda, 53

Ideal principles and pragmatism, 129
identity, 28, 37; definition, 6; and American Indian literature, 26; and authenticity debate, 27, 45; and territory, 29; and strategies of writing and representation, 31; and blood, 33; and resources, 33; politicization of, 34; modification of, 35
*In Search of April Raintree* (Culleton), 55
*In the Spirit of Crazy Horse* (Matthiessen), 8
Indian, use of term as signifier, 29

Indian Allotment Act of 1904, 89
Indian Claims Commission Act of 1946, 33
*Indian Lawyer, The* (Welch), 101, 105, 106, 110
Indian Reorganization Act, 37
Indian Self-Determination Act, 15
Indian Trade and Intercourse Act of 1834, 33
individuality, 22
integration, 9, 11, 16
intellectual sovereignty, 25, 26, 72
intercultural relations and higher education, 14
irony and American Indian identity, 37
isolation and higher education, 14
*I Tell You Now* (Durham), 72

Jaimes, Annette, 82, 83, 87, 162 n. 12
Joseph, Oregon, 24

Kafka, Franz, 153
Kaw Indians, 93
Keats, John, 3
Kerr-McGee, 8
Kingston, Maxine Hong, 77
"known and recognized": as identity criterion, 28; as replacement for blood quantum, 33; definition, 34
Kroeber, Karl, 26
Krupat, Arnold, 161 n. 7; and theory, 26; definition of American Indian literature, 28; and authenticity debate, 43; and storytelling, 84

Language, 21, 22
Lawrence, D. H., 23
LeGuin, Ursula, 51
Lincoln, Kenneth, 25, 27
linear thinking, 59
Linton, Patricia, 52
Littlefield, Daniel F., 43, 159 n. 4
*Lonesome Dove* (McMurtry), 37
*Love Medicine* (Erdrich), 81, 84, 86

Magalener, Marvin, 162 n. 13
Magnus, Bernd, 60
majority culture, 3
"Man Made of Words, The" (Momaday), 22
Maristuen-Rodakowski, Julie, 90
Mathiessen, Peter, 8
McFee, Malcolm, 111, 164 n. 13
McKenzie, Ian, 135
McMurtry, Larry, 37
Melville, Herman, 126
metaphysics and relationship of history to science, 67
*Métis*, 30, 90, 101
Mexican-Americans and American Indian identity, 33
minimalizing: and James Welch, 124; and Fredric Jameson, 126
mixed-blood: origin of term, 30; as literary trope, 37; and authenticity debate, 43; and Louise Erdrich, 87; and Chippewa Indians, 90; and intermarriage, 92; and Mojave Indians, 92
modernism in American Indian literature, 19, 104

Momaday, N. Scott: "The Man Made of Words," 22; and autobiography, 26, 77; *The Ancient Child*, 44; *House Made of Dawn*, 44, 140; and modernism, 104; and pragmatism, 140
Mormons, 64–65
Mourning Dove, 37
multiculturalism, 17, 53
Mystery, the Great, 3

*Names, The* (Momaday), 77
naming: and humor, 27; and strategies of writing and representation, 28; and Gros Ventres, 29; and territory, 29
National Indian Education Association (NIE), 32
*Native American Renaissance* (Lincoln), 25
Navajo Community College, 11
negative capability: definition, 3, 23; and social problems, 18; and choice, 23; and stereotypes, 23; and imagination, 24; and capitalism, 25; and Forbes-Krupat debate, 28; and postapocalypse theory, 38; and academic publishing, 41; and authenticity debate, 48, 147
"Neon Scars" (Rose), 72
*Neuromancer* (Gibson), 52
new criticism, 154
North Dakota Indians, 90
Noyes, A. J., 78, 139

Odiano, Patrick, 49

"Only Approved Indians Can Play:
Made in USA" (Forbes), 36
ontology, 11, 12
*Opposing Self, The* (Trilling), 23
oppression, 17
oral tradition: compared to written
tradition, 14; and individuality,
22; and postmodern tribal views,
45
Osage Indians, 34
*Other Solitudes: Canadian Multi-
cultural Fictions* (Hutcheon and
Richmond), 53
outsiders and American Indian literature, 27
Owens, Louis, 23, 26, 104

Pedagogy and American Indian
women writers, 81
Peltier, Leonard, 7
Pentagon involvement in Black
Hills, S.D., 8
philosophy: as link between cultures, 6; of social integration, 10;
in tribal colleges, 11; and American Indian values, 17
plains Indians, 85
Posner, Richard, 125
postapocalypse theory, 160 n. 6;
description of American Indians,
18; primary principles of, 19;
and negative capability, 38; and
*Love Medicine*, 101–2; and *Tracks*,
101–2; and *The Indian Lawyer*,
102; and genocide, 144
postmodern condition, 6, 22, 24
postmodernism, 145

post-traumatic stress and American
Indian experience, 74
pragmatism, 63, 129–43
Pratt, Scott L., 131
Public Broadcasting System and
minority education, 13

Rabinow, Paul, 86
race and behavioral determinism,
30
racial classification, 30
Rainwater, Catherine, 24, 29, 92
*Red Earth, White Lies* (Deloria),
67
Richmond, Marion, 53
Riesman, David, 111, 164 n. 12
Rodriguez, Richard, 77
Rorty, Richard, 137
Rose, Wendy, 72, 82

Sacred Hoop, The (Allen), 81
Sand Creek Massacre, 50
scapegoating and genocide, 61
Scheick, William J., 37
Schneider, Mary Jane, 90
*Shattering the Silences* (film), 13, 15
Silko, Leslie Marmon: and autobi-
ography, 71–72; and gossip, 86;
criticism of *The Beet Queen*, 101;
and pragmatism, 136–37, 140–41;
and Louise Erdrich, 142
Simpson, Louis, 71, 73
*Slash* (Armstrong), 54–55
Smith, Gary, 116
social transformation and academic
achievement, 12
*Sounding Differences: Conversations*

*with Seventeen Canadian Women Writers* (Williamson), 54
Stannard, David, 49, 146
stereotype: effects on university students, 5; escape from, 14; and cultural background, 22; and negative capability, 23; of American Indians, 23, 24; and improper use of imagination, 24; redescription of, 24; and American Indian studies, 85
*Storm from Paradise: The Politics of Jewish Memory* (Boyarin), 49
storytelling, 84, 86; as counterbalance to mainstream rhetoric, 9; as coping strategy, 39; and *Tracks*, 97

Teachers, 10, 12
teaching, 5, 6
temporal unification of past, present, future, 18, 48, 64, 87
tenure, 13, 14
*Thresholds of Difference: Feminist Critique, Native Women's Writings, Postcolonial Theory* (Emberley), 55
Toelken, Barre, 26
tokenism, 9, 13
*Touching the World* (Eakin), 77
*Tracks* (Erdrich), 89, 90
tradition and Pueblo cultures, 45
tribal colleges, 15, 16
*Tribal Secrets: Recovering American Indian Intellectual Traditions* (Warrior), 26
Trilling, Lionel, 23, 47

*Turn to the Native, The* (Krupat), 43–44

Underground Reservation (Wilson), 34
Union Carbide, 8
Unrau, William, 93
urban Indians, 34

Velie, Alan R., 112
Victorian standard and American Indian women, 80
Vizenor, Gerald: and American Indian identity, 37; *Griever*, 37; *Dead Voices*, 45; *The Heirs of Columbus*, 45; and postmodern tribal views, 45; and colonization, 49; and anthropocentrism, 51
*Voice in the Margin, The* (Krupat), 28

Wallace, Bronwen, 56
*Warrior* (film), 8
Warrior, Robert: and American Indian literature, 26; and Vine Deloria Jr., 59, 129; and autobiography, 72; and Wendy Rose, 72; and Paula Gunn Allen, 82
Weeks, Willie, 116
Welch, James: and American Indian identity, 37; *The Death of Jim Loney*, 37, 44, 109–10; *Winter in the Blood*, 44, 105, 106–7; and modernism, 104; *The Indian Lawyer*, 105, 106, 110; and pragmatism, 141
West, Cornel, 134

Westinghouse, 8

Wetzel, Don, 116–17

*White Man's Indian, The* (Berkhofer), 24, 31

*Wicazo Sa Review*, 28

Wiesel, Elie, 148

Wild, Peter, 112

Williamson, Janice, 54

Wilson, Dick, 8

Wilson, Terry, 34

Windy Boy-Pease, Janine, 96

*Winter in the Blood* (Welch): as second-stage novel, 44; critical reception of, 105; and autobiography, 106–7

*Winters v. United States* and Fort Belknap Reservation, 124

*Woman Warrior, The* (Kingston), 77

Woodard, Charles, 56

Wounded Knee, S.D., 8

written tradition compared to oral tradition, 14

LIBRARY OF CONGRESS CATALOGING-IN-PUBLICATION DATA

LARSON, SIDNER J., 1949–

CAPTURED IN THE MIDDLE : TRADITION AND EXPERIENCE IN

CONTEMPORARY NATIVE AMERICAN WRITING / SIDNER LARSON.

P. CM.

"A MCLELLAN BOOK."

INCLUDES BIBLIOGRAPHICAL REFERENCES AND INDEX.

ISBN 0-295-97904-6 (ACID FREE PAPER)

1. AMERICAN LITERATURE — INDIAN AUTHORS — HISTORY AND

CRITICISM — THEORY, ETC.    2. AMERICAN LITERATURE —

20TH CENTURY — HISTORY AND CRITICISM — THEORY, ETC.    3. INDIANS

OF NORTH AMERICA — INTELLECTUAL LIFE.    4. GROUP IDENTITY

IN LITERATURE.    5. EXPERIENCE IN LITERATURE.    6. INDIANS

IN LITERATURE.    I. TITLE.

PS153.I52 L37 1999

810.9'897 — DC21

99-048431